Wilbur Cross High School LMC
Officially Withdrawn from Collection

—PEOPLE TO KNOW—

HENRY CISNEROS
Building a Better America

Carmen Bredeson

ENSLOW PUBLISHERS, INC.
44 Fadem Road   P.O. Box 38
Box 699   Aldershot
Springfield, N.J. 07081   Hants GU12 6BP
U.S.A.   U.K.

Copyright ©1995 by Carmen Bredeson

All rights reserved.

No part of this book may be reproduced by any means without the written permission of the publisher.

Library of Congress Cataloging-in-Publication Data:

Bredeson, Carmen.
    Henry Cisneros: building a better America / Carmen Bredeson.
        p. cm. — (People to know)
    Includes bibliographical references (p.) and index.
    ISBN 0-89490-546-5
    1. Cisneros, Henry—Juvenile literature. 2. Cabinet officers—United States—Biography—Juvenile literature. 3. Mayors—Texas—San Antonio—Biography—Juvenile literature. [1. Cisneros, Henry. 2. Mayors. 3. Cabinet officers. 4. Mexican Americans—Biography.]
I. Title. II. Series.
E840.8.C52B74   1995
353.85'092—dc20   94-41906
[B]   CIP
                                                                   AC

Printed in the United States of America

10 9 8 7 6 5 4 3 2 1

Illustration Credits:
Institute of Texas Cultures, p. 80; *San Antonio Express-News* Collection, Institute of Texas Cultures, pp. 4, 70, 113; *The San Antonio Light* Collection, Institute of Texas Cultures, pp. 38, 46, 49, 52, 55, 57, 59, 63, 66, 68, 73, 103; United States Department of Housing and Urban Development, p. 87; Zintgraff Collection, Institute of Texas Cultures, pp. 14, 20, 23, 26.

Cover Illustration:
The San Antonio Light Collection, Institute of Texas Cultures

Contents

1 Swearing-in Ceremony 5
2 Childhood 10
3 High School and Texas A&M 18
4 Washington and Politics 31
5 Mayor Cisneros 41
6 Growth in San Antonio 51
7 Exit From Politics 64
8 Private Citizen 75
9 Housing and Urban Development . . . 84
10 Sorting Out the Problems at HUD . . 92
11 Solutions 100
12 The Future? 107
   Chronology 115
   Chapter Notes 117
   Further Reading 125
   Index 126

Henry Cisneros stands in front of the famous Alamo mission in San Antonio, Texas.

1

Swearing-in Ceremony

January 22, 1993, was an important day in the life of forty-five-year-old Henry Cisneros. His nomination as secretary of the U.S. Department of Housing and Urban Development (HUD), had been approved the day before by the United States Senate. Today he would take his place in the East Room of the White House for the swearing-in ceremony, along with the other newly confirmed members of President Bill Clinton's cabinet. Tomorrow he would have to begin to examine the sea of difficulties that HUD needed to address.

HUD was formed in 1965 to help deal with the mounting housing problems that faced the nation's poor. During the preceding few decades, thousands of mostly white, middle- and upper-class families had abandoned their inner-city homes and moved to the suburbs. They were searching for safer streets and a healthier environment in which to raise their children. Left behind were lower-class people who could not afford to move or to repair their homes. The public housing situation in many inner cities deteriorated until it became necessary for the government to intervene, and the cabinet-level department of HUD was created.

Public housing assistance did not begin with the formation of HUD, though. It had its roots in the Great Depression of the 1930s. During the years of the Depression, millions of Americans lost their jobs, and because they could not make the mortgage payments, had to leave their homes. All over the country, homeless people slept wherever they could find shelter. In response to the growing problem, President Franklin Roosevelt signed a bill in 1937 that created the United States Housing Authority. The agency provided subsidies for the construction of low-income housing. Since that time nearly sixty years ago, the federal government has been involved in various forms of public housing assistance.

When the Department of Housing and Urban Development was created in 1965, its director was given cabinet-level status. That enabled the secretary of HUD to be a close associate of the President and also gave the problems of the nation's poor a new importance. The agency's 1993 budget of $35 billion seemed immense, but that money was needed for more than just housing.[1] During recent years, many of America's inner cities had become war zones that were filled with drug dealers, gangs, and thousands of homeless people. There was not enough money in the budget to begin to solve the crisis in our cities. It would take a skillful administrator to decide how the funds could best be spent.

When Henry Cisneros was sworn in by Supreme Court Chief Justice William Rehnquist, the difficulties that faced HUD were passed on to the new secretary. The background and past experiences of Cisneros would be great assets as he began to unravel and understand the maze of HUD's federal assistance programs. His extensive education at Texas A&M, Harvard, and George Washington universities had earned for him a bachelor's and master's degree in Urban Planning, in addition to a master's degree and doctorate in Public Administration.

When Cisneros was nominated to be secretary of HUD in December 1992, President-elect Bill Clinton called the former San Antonio, Texas, mayor "one of the most gifted public servants of our time." Clinton added that "with Henry Cisneros at HUD, America's cities will have the voice and the vision they need and deserve."[2] About Cisneros, former HUD secretary Jack Kemp said: "If there is one man who was born to be HUD Secretary, it was Henry Cisneros. God speed."[3] When his past work was examined, it did seem as if Henry Cisneros had spent his entire career preparing for this new challenge.

As the four-term mayor of San Antonio, Texas,

Cisneros used his years of classroom training to deal with some of the real problems that faced the tenth-largest city in the United States. During his tenure as San Antonio's mayor, he encouraged business and industry to locate in the "Alamo City." More businesses meant an expanded job base for the residents. As more people found work, the city itself began to prosper. With more money in the city coffers, conditions in San Antonio improved and the city began to experience a new prosperity.

The once sleepy, dusty Texas city began to sparkle and started to draw larger numbers of tourists from all over the world. They came to visit the attractive River Walk, with its miles of cobblestone paths lining the meandering San Antonio River. Quaint cafés and shops were interspersed among the beautiful native trees and plants that grew along the waterway. Visitors also explored the ruins of the Alamo and the other historic missions and sites in the area.

San Antonio's increased tourism provided additional revenue that helped pay for such things as school improvements, road construction, and police protection. A more attractive city and a healthier business climate made San Antonio a better place to live and work. Jobs were available that had not been there before and fewer people had to depend on government assistance to pay for their basic needs. As secretary of HUD, maybe Henry Cisneros would have the opportunity to look at his successes in San Antonio and implement some of his ideas on a national level. Once he had an idea, Cisneros seemed to have a talent for getting many different groups to work together and cooperate until his projects became reality.

Henry Cisneros also had another advantage working for him. As an Hispanic American, he knew firsthand about the problems that minorities face in their daily lives. Fortunately for him, Cisneros came from a hardworking family that took advantage of the educational opportunities that were available to them. He overcame many racial barriers that might have discouraged someone else, and in 1981, at the age of thirty-three, he became the first Hispanic-American mayor of a major United States city.

Now, as the secretary of HUD, the problems of not just one city, but the problems of an entire nation of cities waited for Henry Cisneros. Would he have the ability and determination to do what was best for the least fortunate in America? During his confirmation hearing he said:

> I signed on to do this job because I am truly, deeply, personally concerned about the future of our country. I am an optimistic person, and I wake up every morning optimistic, and that optimism sort of buoys me forward. But I am truly and deeply concerned.[4]

As a child and young adult, Henry Cisneros worked hard to succeed at the tasks that were presented to him. Hopefully, that same desire for excellence would follow him as he faced the challenges of his new job.

2

Childhood

When Henry Gabriel Cisneros was born on June 11, 1947, he was the first of George and Elvira Munguia Cisneros's five children. Pauline, George, Jr., Tim, and Tina would follow during the next few years and fill the small home in the Prospect Hills area of San Antonio, Texas. Homework and chores always came before fun and games in the Cisneros household. Henry's parents believed in the value of a good education and tried to instill those ideas in their five children.[1]

The television set was turned off during the week except for news shows and an occasional National Geographic special. On weekends and during the summer, family outings took on the appearance of school field trips, where fun was mixed with learning. Visits to the local museums and the zoo were often used to enrich and entertain the minds of the young Cisneros children. The family attended the symphony and opera and also played various musical instruments at home.

Dinner at the Cisneros home was a special time that was set aside for discussions about interesting school experiences and current events. Often the family would spend several hours around the table, talking about their daily lives and having heated discussions about a variety of topics. After the long dinners, Mr. and Mrs. Cisneros would relax or take a walk while the children cleaned up the kitchen.

Henry's formal education began when he entered first grade at the Little Flower Catholic School. He made very good grades and because of his rapid progress, Henry was allowed to skip third grade entirely and go directly to fourth grade. He had no trouble keeping up with the work, but he was always a year younger than most of his classmates.

Elvira Munguia Cisneros encouraged her children to use their free time constructively. After the house was clean and the grass cut, Henry often spent his extra hours building model airplanes and reading. The father of Elvira Cisneros, Romulo Munguia, supplied his grandchildren with books about Mexico, to make sure that they understood and appreciated their heritage.

Grandfather Munguia's own history was filled with tales of danger and excitement. Both of his parents had died by the time he was eight years old. He had to support himself, so he went to work for a printer in Guadalajara, Mexico. By the time Romulo was fifteen, he had moved to Mexico City and gotten a job in the print shop of a newspaper there. The paper was owned by brothers who were opponents of the then unpopular President of Mexico, Porfirio Díaz. They printed articles that were critical of President Díaz and eventually the police raided the paper and arrested the employees. They were all sentenced to death, but Romulo was later released because he was only eighteen years old.

In his search for political freedom, Munguia eventually fled to the United States in 1926. He got a job at a Spanish-language newspaper in San Antonio and was able to send for his family to join him in America. After working at the newspaper for a few years, Romulo Munguia started his own print shop. It became a place where leaders in the Hispanic-American community often gathered to discuss politics and have campaign literature printed. Henry and his family lived in the same neighborhood where Grandfather Munguia's business was located. Henry spent many hours at the print shop while he was growing up. Often, during those visits, he listened to discussions among the customers about Hispanic-American issues in the San Antonio area.

Henry did not spend all of his hours studying and improving his mind, however. Like a typical child, he spent time outside, running and playing with the other children in the neighborhood. On his street there were sixteen boys who were the same age as Henry. There was an almost continual football or baseball game in progress somewhere on the block. Henry also belonged to a Boy Scout troop and played Little League baseball. When it was his turn to bat, he was cheered on from the sidelines by his family and friends.

Henry was well known in his family for his attention to detail. He sometimes wrote plays for his brothers and sisters and then spent days preparing the costumes and sets for their productions. When he played with his extensive model airplane collection, he first designed complicated runway patterns in the dirt outside. Henry seemed to be able to find interesting ways to spend his time, and the other neighborhood children often joined in the fun.

Henry lived in a middle-class, predominantly Hispanic-American neighborhood. Most of the activities there revolved around the family and the Catholic Church. There were frequent block parties and church socials, and, always, Mass on Sunday morning. Henry has often said that his childhood reminds him of pictures that Norman Rockwell, a popular artist of the time, liked to paint. Rockwell's wonderful pictures were extraordinary scenes of ordinary Americans and their day-to-day activities. Henry Cisneros has said that growing up in his neighborhood "was Norman Rockwell, but all of the faces were brown."[2]

Henry grew up as part of a caring family and a stable

Henry Cisneros played Little League baseball while he was a student at Little Flower Catholic School in San Antonio, Texas.

community. He had intelligent, industrious parents who worked hard to instill values in their children. Mr. Cisneros seemed to be always busy, either improving his mind or the house where his family lived. He took classes at the local college and correspondence courses by mail. He added a room to the house and finished an area in the attic to give his family more space to spread out.

Mrs. Cisneros stayed busy too, educating her children and keeping house for the family. She also was a leader for Boy and Girl Scout troops and was active in the PTA (Parent-Teacher Association) and various church organizations. After her children were grown, Mrs. Cisneros said in an interview: "I think my children are my greatest accomplishment. I think we gave them a good foundation. Up to a certain age you can guide them; after that what they do is a reflection of what they have learned at home."[3] As a result of their parents' efforts, the Cisneros siblings were prepared to take their places in a society that often looked down on Hispanic Americans.

Many Hispanic Americans were not as fortunate as the Cisneros family. In 1960, when Henry was thirteen years old, there were an estimated seven million Hispanic Americans in the United States. Large numbers of them had immigrated from Mexico or Puerto Rico, and many of them were poor and uneducated.[4] Some lived in one-room shacks that had no indoor plumbing or electricity, and they barely made enough money to feed their families. Their lack of skills and education kept many of them trapped in a cycle of poverty. Because few of them voted or had any political power, they were often ignored by those who ran the government.

Henry Cisneros was fortunate to have come from a different background. Even though his ancestors did not have material wealth, they seemed to possess a determination to excel in spite of great odds. Henry's father, George Cisneros, was descended from Spaniards who came to this country in the early 1700s, to help colonize the New World. As the decades passed, the family continued to grow until their farm in New Mexico became too small to support everyone. Many in the Cisneros family had to move away from the original land grant and look for new ways to make a living.

Henry's father was born into a family of migrant farm workers. These were laborers who moved from place to place and harvested various crops for the farmers who owned the land. The entire migrant family, including the children, worked very hard and received only minimal wages. It was very difficult for the children to attend school because, when the crops were ready to harvest, everyone had to work. Even though George Cisneros worked in the fields from the age of nine, he was apparently determined to get an education and found a way to go to school. Even though staying in school was difficult for George, he eventually became the first member of his family to graduate from high school. He later went on to business school and then into the Army, where he rose to the rank of colonel by the time he retired in 1976.

Education played an important role in the lives of both the Munguia and Cisneros families. Even though they were not wealthy, their knowledge empowered them far more than money ever could. Education opened doors for many of the members of Henry's family, doors that were still closed to many other Hispanic Americans.

3

High School
and Texas A&M

Henry finished the eighth grade at Little Flower and, at age thirteen, moved on to Central Catholic High School, an all-boys school in San Antonio. During his years at Central, he played the French horn in the band, ran on the cross-country track team and joined the Reserve Officer Training Corps (ROTC). The ROTC was a student organization that introduced its members to military philosophy and discipline. The boys who belonged to the organization wore uniforms to their meetings and learned to march and follow the ROTC officer's orders.

One day, during Henry's junior year, all eight hundred of the students at Central were allowed to walk a few blocks away to witness a special event. President and Mrs. John F. Kennedy were making a tour of Texas and were scheduled to arrive in San Antonio on November 21, 1963. Their motorcade would travel through the city before the President continued on to Dallas the next day. The students at Henry's school were among the thousands of people who lined the streets to wave at the handsome young President and his beautiful wife as they waved to the crowd. It was an exciting event to watch, and was the topic of much discussion as the boys slowly walked back to school.

During the next afternoon, classes were interrupted for an important announcement. The students listened to the tragic news that President Kennedy had been shot and killed as his motorcade made its way through the streets of Dallas, Texas. The nation was stunned by the assassination. The tragedy was even more pronounced for the boys at Central, because they had just seen President Kennedy the day before, as he waved and smiled in their direction. Henry Cisneros expressed his feelings in a poem that he wrote about the November tragedy.

The years passed and, in addition to his school work and extracurricular activities, Henry had his eye on a special girl. She attended Providence High School, the Catholic all-girl's school that was located across the street from Central. Her name was Mary Alice Perez and she came from a family of nine children. Henry and Mary Alice got better acquainted when they saw each other at football games and school dances. They never actually

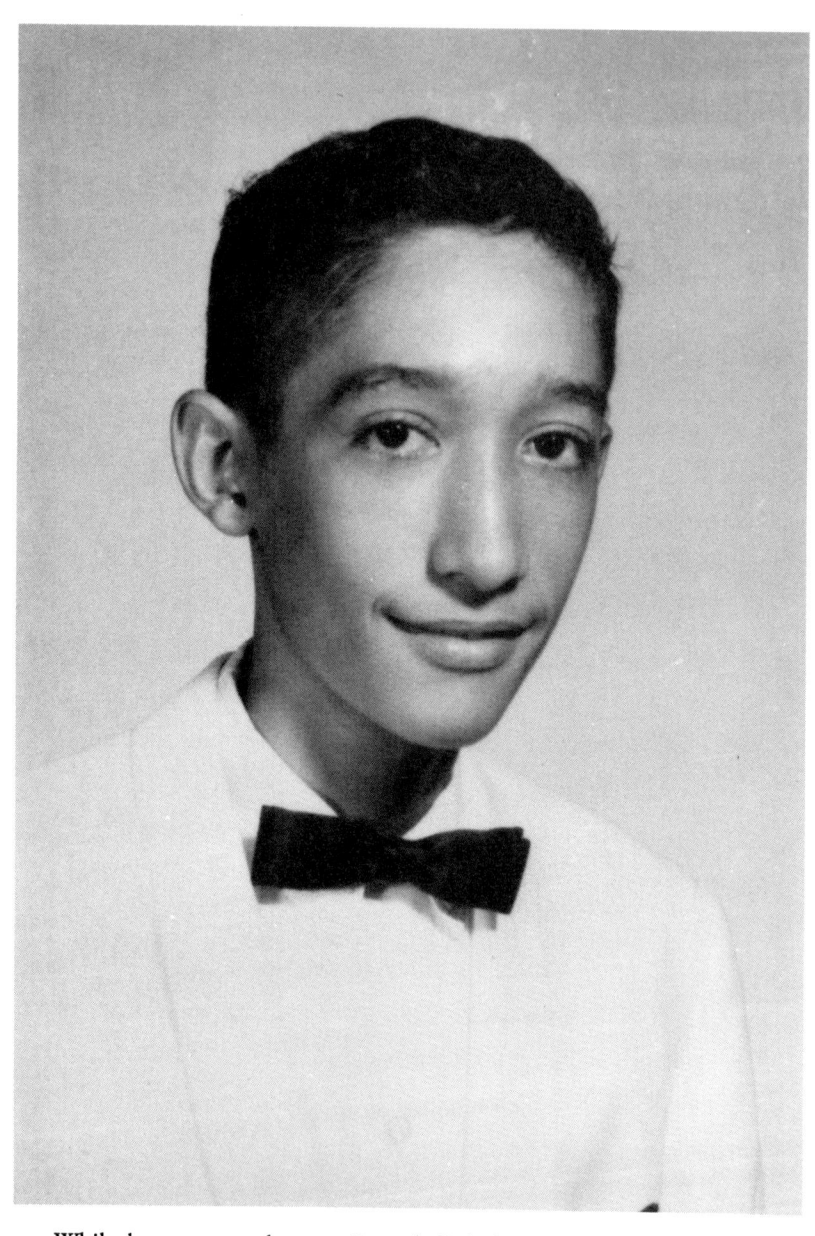

While he was a student at Central Catholic High School, Henry played the French horn in the band and belonged to the ROTC.

went out on a date until Henry's senior year because Mary Alice's parents were very strict and she was two years younger than Henry. After they began to date, their romance blossomed and Mary Alice was Henry's date for his senior prom.

With his high school years drawing to a close, Henry Cisneros had to make some decisions about his future. A career in the military interested him very much. His own father was a member of the Army Reserves and San Antonio was the home of five large military bases. Henry had grown up around airplanes and men in uniform. The skies over his Texas home were full of aircraft and, as a boy, Henry had spent many hours building models of the airplanes he saw flying overhead.

With a career as a pilot in mind, Henry decided to apply for admission to the Air Force Academy in Colorado Springs, Colorado. Much to his disappointment, he was turned down because he was only sixteen years old and weighed just one hundred and thirty-five pounds. He was advised to apply in another year or two, after he was older and had gained a little weight.

Henry was now in search of another college to attend. He selected Texas A&M in College Station, Texas, a university that was founded in 1871 as a military institution. By the time Henry entered as a freshman in 1964, A&M, which stands for Agricultural and Mechanical, was no longer primarily a military school, but the ROTC, called the Corps of Cadets, was still an important part of campus life.

Texas A&M in 1964 was a school steeped in tradition and it was a rather unusual choice for an Hispanic American. A&M was a predominantly white, all-male school, that was known for its gung-ho Corps of Cadets. Very few minorities attended A&M, and women students were not admitted until 1963, the same year that mandatory participation in the Corps was dropped. Henry Cisneros said later that "the worst place I could have selected to go to college as an Hispanic in the sixties was A&M." He added, that "at A&M there is no place for you except the one you make for yourself."[1]

In spite of the fact that he was definitely outnumbered by his white classmates, Henry quickly got involved in campus life and began to make a place for himself. He joined the Aggie Band and the Corps of Cadets during his freshman year. He said that "I got up there and got elected to a class office and was named outstanding cadet in my unit and I got into the A&M swing of things."[2] By the end of his sophomore year, he was selected to be the sergeant major of the Aggie Band. (Students at Texas A&M were nicknamed the "Aggies.")

It was during his sophomore year that Cisneros experienced an unusual defeat—he failed a class. He called his mother and said "Mama, I'm going to leave school and join the Green Berets, because I'm a failure! I got an F in calculus!"[3] Cisneros did not leave school, but

Henry Cisneros was a member of the Corps of Cadets during his years at Texas A&M University.

decided instead to change his major from aeronautical engineering to city management. His own city of San Antonio was a good example of what was wrong with much of America.

Most sections of San Antonio were comfortable, well-maintained neighborhoods that were home to middle- and upper-class residents. Prospect Hills, Cisneros's own neighborhood, was a nice place to live, with its small, neat houses that were surrounded by trimmed yards. But, just a few blocks away, the city's lower class lived in dismal shacks that had no plumbing or electricity. The streets there were little more than dirt paths that flooded every time there was rain and sent garbage and sewage flowing into the yards.

San Antonio was not the only city in America that had a serious housing problem with its poor residents. Mayors and city councils all over the country were looking for ways to deal with the growing numbers of unemployed people who lived in squalor in some sections of the inner cities. Universities had begun to establish departments of urban planning in an attempt to educate students about the problem. Henry Cisneros enrolled in just such a program at Texas A&M. Cisneros's dreams of a career in the military faded as he studied the problems that his new courses presented.

During his junior year, Henry Cisneros was selected to attend a meeting at the U.S. Military Academy in West Point, New York. Exceptional students from across the country were there for a Conference on United States Affairs. While he sat in on the meetings, Cisneros discovered that he knew far less about the workings of the country than did many of the students from the East Coast schools. He later said: "I was totally outclassed. We sat around the conference table and I never opened my mouth."[4] After the conference, Henry returned to A&M, determined to study hard so that he could gain a deeper understanding about the complexities of the federal government and its programs.

Life at A&M also included other activities that did not involve classes and study. Football was a popular part of campus life, and the cadets liked to show their girlfriends off during the games. Mary Alice came from San Antonio to join Henry for an occasional football weekend. During an Aggie game, all of the members of the Corps of Cadets and their dates stood during the entire four quarters. It was a school tradition that was religiously observed, one that often left the girls with aching feet from their high heel shoes.

In addition to his other activities, Cisneros played intramural basketball and football, jogged, and belonged to many organizations on campus. In fact, his schedule was so busy that he usually only got five or six hours of sleep a night. His hard work and dedication paid off though and, during his senior year, Henry Cisneros was selected to be the commander of the 300-member Aggie Band. It was the highest honor in the Corps of Cadets.

As a member of ROTC, Cisneros participated in various field training exercises.

Henry's Hispanic-American background had not prevented him from achieving a great deal during his college years. Later he would look back and say: "If you could perform in the classroom, if your military performance was up to speed, if you had leadership capabilities, then there was no limit."[5] Dennis Parrish, one of Henry's college roommates said:

> I always figured that politics was the direction he'd end up going. He was so gung-ho and worked so hard on the things that seemed to be important in gaining leadership in the Corps of Cadets. He practiced being a leader even before we were allowed to be leaders.[6]

In the spring of 1968, Henry Cisneros graduated from Texas A&M with a bachelor's degree in Regional and Urban Planning. He decided to remain at the university and work on a master's degree in the same field. He was awarded a scholarship that helped to pay for his expenses while he continued his education. There was so much more to learn about the mounting problems that faced America's cities.

Henry Cisneros continued to attend classes at A&M while working as an assistant to the city manager of Bryan, Texas, a small town nearby. He also served an internship in the San Antonio city manager's office. During his second year of graduate school, Henry got involved in the Model Cities Program, which was established by Congress in 1966 at the urging of President Lyndon Johnson.

In 1964, President Johnson asked Congress for $962 million to fight a war against poverty. The President was concerned about the growing numbers of poor people in America, and he addressed the problem in his 1965 State of the Union address. He said: "unfortunately many Americans live on the outskirts of hope—some because of their poverty, and some because of their color, and all too many because of both."[7] The Model Cities Act was an experimental program that was designed to provide federal money to help revitalize one hundred and fifty inner cities in the United States.

During 1965, at Johnson's request, Congress also created the Department of Housing and Urban Development (HUD), where Henry Cisneros would serve nearly thirty years later. The cabinet-level department would administer federal funds that were set aside to build low-income housing and provide rental assistance to the needy.

San Antonio was one of the cities chosen to participate in President Johnson's Model Cities Program. Nearly a billion dollars was to be divided among the one hundred and fifty localities, to help them improve living conditions in their poorest neighborhoods. The Model Cities Office in San Antonio was located right across the street from the Munguia print shop, where Cisneros had spent many happy hours as a child. In his new job with the Model Cities Program, Cisneros listened to people's concerns about unpaved streets, underfunded schools, and poor city services. He had heard many of those same complaints expressed when he visited the print shop during his childhood.

The Model Cities Program called for neighborhood councils to be formed, groups that were made up of residents from the community as well as civic leaders. Meetings were held so that citizens could discuss their concerns and look for solutions to their problems. The meetings often continued far into the night and Henry Cisneros was always right there, listening and taking notes. Only now he did not have to just listen. Now he could do something about the concerns of the people.

As part of the Model Cities Program, Cisneros was able to take the recommendations of the neighborhood councils to the City Council and mayor's office. They, in turn, discussed the requests and appropriated some of the federal funds that were at their disposal. Many of the problems that had plagued the neighborhoods for years could now be taken care of. Henry Cisneros was able to put his education to use and start to help the poorest people in his city.

In January 1969, twenty-one-year-old Henry Cisneros was named the assistant director for the Model Cities Program in San Antonio. He later said that "everything I know about citizen participation and the mechanics of making government work, I learned during those Model City years."[8]

Another important event also occurred in 1969. On June 1, Mary Alice Perez and Henry Cisneros were married in St. Agnes Catholic Church in San Antonio. The couple rented a small apartment and, while Mary Alice worked in a bank, Henry finished up the final research paper for his master's degree and went to work full-time for the Model Cities Program.

During the time that he was trying to help San Antonio solve some of its worst problems, Cisneros began to contemplate the need for yet more education. He had learned a great deal about urban planning, but he still wanted to know more about administration and finance. Also, maybe he needed to look at a different area of the country to get another perspective on the problems of the cities. With all of those goals in mind, he applied to and was accepted in a doctoral program at George Washington University, located in Washington, D.C.

4

Washington and Politics

After a great deal of discussion, Mary Alice and Henry Cisneros decided to leave their Texas home and head for the East Coast. The 2,000-mile-trip from San Antonio to Washington was a real adventure in their old, packed-to-the-roof Volkswagen. Mary Alice had never been away from home and the farther they went, the colder the weather got. When they arrived at their destination they had to stay with friends because they did not yet have a place to live.

Henry and Mary Alice looked at several apartments and selected the only one that they could afford, a tiny place that was located a few blocks from the Capitol. They were unfamiliar with the area and the employment opportunities, but both of them needed to find a job to help cover expenses. Within a short time, Mary Alice found a job in a bank and Henry went for an interview at an organization called the National League of Cities (NLC).

The interview went well and, instead of the part-time job that he wanted, Cisneros was offered a full-time position at the NLC. Cisneros would manage to work at both his job and his doctorate at the same time. Allen Pritchard, the number two man at the NLC, said: "I've never worked with anybody who used his time more effectively than Henry did. I came to rely on him totally because the quality of his work was so high."[1]

Cisneros's work days were usually very long, between his duties at NLC and his schoolwork. He had learned how to cram a lot of activities into a small amount of time while he was a student at A&M. In Washington, he also found the hours to fulfill all of his work and class assignments. He often had to travel with his job too, and it was during one of his trips that he missed an important event. While Henry Cisneros was away on business, Mary Alice gave birth to the couple's first child, a daughter they named Teresa. Henry's brother George was in Washington for a visit, and so was able to be with Mary Alice to welcome the new baby.

During the second year that the family was in Washington, Cisneros applied to be a White House Fellow. The program, which was started by President Richard Nixon, provided an opportunity for a few qualified young men and women to work closely with top government officials for a year. There were three thousand applications for the sixteen positions that were available.

Henry Cisneros received one of those few appointments, and he was assigned to work with Elliot Richardson, who was then secretary of Health, Education and Welfare (HEW). As a member of President Richard Nixon's cabinet, Richardson had many important meetings to attend and duties to perform. Cisneros did research for his boss and went with him to congressional hearings. Through this close work with Richardson, Cisneros gained valuable insights into the workings of the United States government at the highest levels.

In an interview years later, Elliot Richardson said that Henry Cisneros:

> . . . had an extraordinary combination of assets: intelligence, diligence, charm, an attractive personality and a deep interest in public issues. I recall telling him on one occasion that I regarded him as a national resource and that I hoped he would pursue the additional education and experience to prepare himself for a life in public service.[2]

When his year as a White House Fellow drew to a close, Cisneros decided to take Richardson's advice. He made plans to go to Harvard University, to the John F. Kennedy School of Government, to get another degree.

He had completed all of the courses at George Washington University that were necessary for his doctorate. All he had left to do was write his dissertation, a book-length analysis about some aspect of his studies. He did not have to remain in Washington in order to finish the dissertation, and he did complete it at a later date.

Mary Alice and Henry Cisneros packed their belongings, and along with their two-year-old daughter Teresa, moved to Boston, Massachusetts. As usual, the couple did not have much money, so they had to rent a very small apartment. Cisneros had been awarded a Ford Foundation grant to study at Harvard, but it only provided $10,000, and that amount had to last for two years. When he was asked to teach part-time at MIT, the Massachusetts Institute of Technology, he jumped at the chance to make a little money. Mary Alice also found a job and a day care center for Teresa, so the family was able to move into a larger apartment.

The two years in Boston passed quickly and soon Henry Cisneros was faced with new decisions. He was nearly twenty-seven years old and was the father of one child with another one expected soon. He had graduate degrees from some of the most prestigious universities in the country. Cisneros had spent all of his adult life preparing for a career in city management. Now seemed like the perfect time to go home and get to work. When the University of Texas at San Antonio offered him a teaching position in the Division of Environmental Studies, he was quick to accept it. Henry, Mary Alice, and Teresa Cisneros were about to return to San Antonio.

Once again, Henry and Mary Alice packed the same old Volkswagen and prepared to move. This time though, they were headed home to familiar surroundings and to the people who loved them. San Antonio was a curious mixture in the 1970s. It had the appearance of a sleepy village in spite of a population of over five hundred thousand people. The city was experiencing a period of rapid growth and a substantial increase in population. Unfortunately, there were not enough jobs for all of the people who moved to San Antonio.

In an article that he later wrote, Henry Cisneros said about San Antonio in the 1970s:

> We began to realize that vaguely charming wasn't enough to carry our city into the next decade, much less the next century.... We needed a more business-based economy. We needed jobs that brought a promise of an improved standard of living. We needed plants and factories to improve the woefully inadequate tax base in our school districts.[3]

The local government was controlled by powerful, white businesspeople, while the more than 50 percent Hispanic-American population had little or no voice in the decisions that affected their daily lives.

Historically, city council members had been elected to at-large positions. That meant that candidates for the council seats could live anywhere within the San Antonio city limits. Several council members might even live in the same neighborhood, while large sections of the city had no elected representatives. Since the white population turned out in greater numbers to vote than did the Hispanic Americans and African Americans, the white candidates usually defeated their minority challengers at the polls.

An undercurrent of unrest was beginning to rumble through the town. Representatives of the Hispanic-American interests had started to exert pressure on City Hall to address the problems of the minority community. In 1973, Ernesto Cortes founded Communities Organized for Public Service (COPS). The organization was formed to involve local people in the affairs of their government. Cortes enlisted the help of community volunteers and leaders from the neighborhood churches and civic organizations. They helped educate minority residents about their rights and encouraged their participation in the local governing process.

Those traditionally in control in San Antonio did not want to see their power base erode, so they resisted the efforts of the newcomers. The Hispanic-American and white communities were sharply divided on the issue of equal representation. Into this controversy stepped

Henry Cisneros, a highly educated, articulate, and experienced Hispanic American. Conditions were ripe for the entrance of Cisneros into the arena of San Antonio politics.

Shortly after his return to San Antonio, twenty-seven-year-old Henry Cisneros decided to run for a seat on the city council. His campaign was one long media event. He appeared all over town, giving speeches and serving barbecue to the crowds that gathered to meet him. He spoke clearly and intelligently to his audiences and won the support of many San Antonio voters, Hispanic and white alike. Even though he was a Hispanic American, he did not represent a threat to the status quo.

With the help of family, friends, and his own charisma, Henry Cisneros won his 1975 race for city council with 52 percent of the votes. He was the youngest person ever elected to serve on the San Antonio City Council. Just one month after his election, a second daughter, named Mercedes, was born to Henry and Mary Alice. Cisneros had a beautiful family, was living in the city of his birth, and was in a position to make an impact on the quality of life in his hometown.

It did not take him long to get to work. He once said that "I'm a hands-on guy. I have to be in a situation, feel it, smell it, before I can understand it."[4] He got out into the community and talked to the people and learned for himself where the problems were. Members of the San

Students listen to Henry Cisneros while he was a member of the San Antonio City Council in 1976.

Antonio media followed him around and recorded his every move.

Cisneros received a lot of TV air time and space in the local newspapers, and the public got to know their newest council member very well. They apparently liked what they saw because Henry Cisneros was elected to a second term on the city council. He seemed to serve as a bridge between the white and Hispanic-American communities. Maybe all the people of San Antonio could now join together to make the city a better place for everyone.

It was during his second council term that Henry and Mary Alice Cisneros bought their first house. It was the small, two-bedroom house that Grandfather Munguia had owned more than fifty years before. Henry and his family chose to remain in their old neighborhood, among familiar people and places, rather than settle in one of the newer San Antonio suburbs. It was the rapid growth of those suburbs that prompted a political battle in San Antonio, a battle that concerned adequate representation for all areas of town.

In 1976, the United States Department of Justice ruled that the voting procedure in San Antonio was unfair to minorities. They advised the San Antonio City Council that they could either adopt a policy of single-member districts, or fight the Justice Department ruling in court. Henry Cisneros was a strong supporter of the single-member district method of electing council members, and he actively campaigned for its passage. After much heated debate, the proposal narrowly passed. As a result, San Antonio was divided into ten city council voting districts.

Under the new rules, one representative from each of the ten districts was to be elected by the voters who lived in that district. This gave the candidates in minority neighborhoods an opportunity to run for a seat on the city council and actually have a chance to be elected. The people in each of the ten districts could only vote for the candidates in their district and not for people running for any of the other nine positions.

In the 1977 election, the first held under the new single-member district rule, Hispanic Americans won five seats on the city council and an African American was elected to one. The office of mayor was still open to candidates from anywhere in the city; the mayor had one vote. That made a total of eleven possible votes on council matters. For the first time in the history of San Antonio, minority council members had a majority of the vote.

Henry Cisneros served on the city council for a total of six years, or three terms. During his tenure, he gained valuable experience in the workings of city government and became a familiar and popular figure around San Antonio. With the 1981 elections on the horizon, Cisneros had some difficult decisions to make. Would he run for another council term, a race that he was sure to win? Or, would he take a chance and run for mayor?

5

Mayor Cisneros

After many discussions with advisors and members of his family, Henry Cisneros announced that he would be a candidate for mayor in the 1981 election. A flurry of activity followed his decision. During his years in public office, Cisneros got to know many of the people in San Antonio and had accumulated a list of possible supporters. Some of these people were eager to participate in the campaign, and they helped to enlist others who were also interested in having Cisneros as their mayor.

Public appearances were a key element in the campaign of Henry Cisneros. He had usually performed well in front of the cameras and he had an easy rapport with crowds of people. He used those talents to his advantage and scheduled appearances all over San

Antonio. He gave speeches in Spanish in the Hispanic-American neighborhoods and talks about the economic future of the city to the business community. He held news conferences and issued press releases on a regular basis.

The news media followed Cisneros around, ready to capture his magic for their evening broadcasts, and he led them on a merry chase from one end of the city to the other. At one rally, just before it was time for the voters to go to the polls, Cisneros said to the audience: "Now is the time, compadres [friends]. If on the day after the election I hear you saying, 'Poor Henry, if only I had known you needed my help,' I think I will cry."[1] In the end, Henry Cisneros did not have to shed any tears. He easily defeated John Steen, a millionaire white businessperson, and won the election with 61.8 percent of the vote. At the age of thirty-three, Henry Cisneros became the first Hispanic-American mayor of a major U.S. city and the youngest mayor in San Antonio's history.

On the day after the election Mayor Cisneros was a guest on the nationally televised *Today Show*. During the following weeks, he was interviewed by journalists from all over the world and appeared on many TV and radio programs. Successful Hispanic-American politicians were uncommon, and many people wanted to speak with Cisneros about his agenda for the coming years. In all of the interviews, Henry Cisneros kept repeating the same clear message. He was there to promote his city. He said that San Antonio is "the place in the sun for new businesses to start and for old businesses to relocate and for tourists to enjoy themselves."[2]

San Antonio, the city that Mayor Cisneros was to govern for at least the next two years, had a long and colorful history. Explorers from Spain settled in the area early in the eighteenth century and established a string of missions along the San Antonio River. One of the missions, founded in 1718, later came to be called the Alamo. In 1836, it was the scene of an historic thirteen-day battle in the Texas fight for independence from Mexico. For many years after that battle, the Alamo lay in ruins.

Then in 1849 the United States Army leased the old mission from the Catholic Church and repaired the buildings. The structures were used to house troops and store food and supplies. By 1870, all of the United States Army troops in Texas were headquartered in San Antonio and the population of the town had risen to 12,000 people.[3]

When Henry Cisneros became mayor, the "Alamo City" had a population of 800,000. Many of the city's historic buildings had become tourist attractions. The San Antonio Conservation Society, founded in 1924, was responsible for the preservation of many historic sites around the city. The military also continued to play a major role in the economy of the city. Five bases were located in the surrounding area and they provided employment opportunities for many San Antonio residents. The city's economy depended heavily on both the military and tourist industries.

In 1981, the year that Henry Cisneros became mayor, only 12 percent of the jobs in San Antonio were in the manufacturing area. The average income of the residents was lower than the incomes earned by people in comparably sized cities. San Antonio had a 53 percent Hispanic-American population, and many in that ethnic minority were living below the poverty level.[4]

During his mayoral campaign, Henry Cisneros hammered away at the importance of economic development. He was elected by low-income voters but he rarely asked for more government social programs. Instead, he thought that growth in the private economy would help his constituents most.[5] He was a great advocate of small business and presented some statistics from a 1981 MIT study to support his views. The analysis said that "nearly 2/3 of all American jobs created between 1969 and 1976 stemmed from firms employing less than 20 people."[6]

Cisneros's desire to attract and assist small companies led to the creation of the One Stop Business Center in San Antonio. It was designed to help both existing businesses and new ones who wanted to locate in the Alamo City. The center offered financial assistance and helped find suitable sites on which to build. It also offered simplified methods of obtaining building permits and utility hookups. Generally, lots of "red tape" was eliminated so that new business could move into San Antonio and old ones could expand with less difficulty.

Early in his first term, Cisneros said: "I can take the initiative, really support something and get it to the point where it will be done—and I start very few things that I don't get done."[7] One of the things that Henry Cisneros began was a campaign to put San Antonio on the map. He went to Washington to meet with President Ronald Reagan. He addressed the Texas Legislature. He courted business representatives who were interested in relocating their company offices. He appeared on television shows and granted dozens of interviews. And everywhere he went, he promoted San Antonio.

He worked twelve-to-fourteen-hour days and wore out his staff—not everyone had as much energy as the new mayor. During his late nights in the office, the Aggie War Hymn, Texas A&M's school song, could sometimes be heard blaring in the background. In addition to his mayoral duties, he still taught classes at the University of Texas at San Antonio. He had to earn some money to support his family, since the job of mayor only paid a little over $4,000 a year. It was supposed to be a largely ceremonial office, but Henry Cisneros turned it into more than a full-time job. He spent a great deal of his time searching for ways to draw industry into the San Antonio area. He reminded his

Mayor Henry Cisneros speaks during a San Antonio City Council meeting.

constituents that "new and expanded businesses means new jobs, better jobs, and a better economy."[8]

In 1982, the National Jaycees named Henry Cisneros one of ten Outstanding Young Men of America. He was selected from a field of 6,000 nominees. He and his family traveled to Oklahoma so that Cisneros could accept the award. When they returned to the San Antonio airport, they were greeted by a mariachi band and cheerleaders, who were there to welcome the popular mayor home. When the music and cheering finally ended, Henry Cisneros addressed the crowd. He said that the trophy he had received in Oklahoma would be on display in City Hall because all of the people of San Antonio were responsible for his winning it.[9]

During that same year of 1981, Cisneros was named by President Reagan to serve on the President's Commission on Federalism. The committee was formed to examine the government's role in providing assistance to cities. At that time, Cisneros said: "These are hard times for cities, and we're seeing only the tip of the iceberg as to how serious things will eventually become."[10]

Henry Cisneros, and many others in San Antonio, had a vision for their city. Several groups began to get together to talk about the future. Eventually more than 2,000 people started to meet regularly, to plan and to dream. The large group was made up of all kinds of people, from every ethnic group and occupation. They formed committees and held town meetings. They studied statistics and argued about what was important for the future of San Antonio. The result of all of their work and debate was a report called "Target '90," which was a list of ninety-three goals for the city to work toward meeting by 1990.

One of the aims was the development of a bioscience park, to attract research and health-related industries to the city. Another goal revolved around the construction of new freeways and roads, to make access easier for new business. An increase in educational standards was also a very important part of "Target '90." For many years Cisneros was especially concerned about the problem of illiteracy in this country. In an article he said: "One out of five Americans can't read. By 1990, one out of every two black 17-year-olds will be labeled a nonreader. At least 15% of all urban high school graduates now cannot read beyond the sixth-grade level."[11]

The "Target '90" group wanted to address the problems of illiteracy and the high dropout rates in the schools. They arranged for successful business and sports figures to appear at the schools and talk to the students about the importance of a good education. They sponsored field trips so that classes could visit various businesses, to find out about how companies run and what kind of training was needed to work there. In addition, career counseling was provided, to give constituents that "new and expanded businesses means new jobs, better jobs, and a better economy."[8]

In 1982, the National Jaycees named Henry Cisneros one of ten Outstanding Young Men of America. He was selected from a field of 6,000 nominees. He and his family traveled to Oklahoma so that Cisneros could accept the award. When they returned to the San Antonio airport, they were greeted by a mariachi band and cheerleaders, who were there to welcome the popular mayor home. When the music and cheering finally ended, Henry Cisneros addressed the crowd. He said that the trophy he had received in Oklahoma would be on display in City Hall because all of the people of San Antonio were responsible for his winning it.[9]

During that same year of 1981, Cisneros was named by President Reagan to serve on the President's Commission on Federalism. The committee was formed to examine the government's role in providing assistance to cities. At that time, Cisneros said: "These are hard times for cities, and we're seeing only the tip of the iceberg as to how serious things will eventually become."[10]

Henry Cisneros, and many others in San Antonio, had a vision for their city. Several groups began to get together to talk about the future. Eventually more than 2,000 people started to meet regularly, to plan and to dream. The large group was made up of all kinds of people, from every ethnic group and occupation. They formed committees and held town meetings. They studied statistics and argued about what was important for the future of San Antonio. The result of all of their work and debate was a report called "Target '90," which was a list of ninety-three goals for the city to work toward meeting by 1990.

One of the aims was the development of a bioscience park, to attract research and health-related industries to the city. Another goal revolved around the construction of new freeways and roads, to make access easier for new business. An increase in educational standards was also a very important part of "Target '90." For many years Cisneros was especially concerned about the problem of illiteracy in this country. In an article he said: "One out of five Americans can't read. By 1990, one out of every two black 17-year-olds will be labeled a nonreader. At least 15% of all urban high school graduates now cannot read beyond the sixth-grade level."[11]

The "Target '90" group wanted to address the problems of illiteracy and the high dropout rates in the schools. They arranged for successful business and sports figures to appear at the schools and talk to the students about the importance of a good education. They sponsored field trips so that classes could visit various businesses, to find out about how companies run and what kind of training was needed to work there. In addition, career counseling was provided, to give

Henry Cisneros spent a great deal of time talking to the media during the fourteen years he held office in San Antonio.

students a look at where the best jobs would be in the future. If Henry Cisneros was any example, education seemed to be a key to success.

As his first term in office drew to a close, Mayor Cisneros had just scratched the surface of his master plan for San Antonio. He had familiarized himself with the procedures that were necessary to get things done. He had also established a good working relationship with most of his associates in city government. Now was not the time to give up. He definitely needed another term in order to turn some of his ideas into reality.

Growth in San Antonio

Henry Cisneros was easily re-elected in 1983, with 94.2 percent of the vote. During his second term in office, his previous two years of hard work began to pay off, and San Antonio started to shine. A large regional grocery chain moved its corporate offices to the city. Money was appropriated to identify and improve some of the historic areas in town. A $400,000 state grant was obtained to build a high school that was dedicated to the study of the technologies of the future. In March 1983, President Reagan presented Mayor Cisneros with the All American City Award at a White House ceremony in Washington, D.C., and in May 1983 the President visited the "Alamo City."

Expressway construction began to improve transportation in and around the San Antonio area, and the convention center was expanded. Cisneros hoped to

Mary Alice, Mercedes, and Teresa Cisneros attend a victory party with Henry Cisneros to celebrate his second mayoral win in 1983.

lure large conventions to the city and provide them with ample opportunities to spend their money. With tourist dollars in mind, the possible construction of a large mall near the river was discussed. Many of San Antonio's ten million visitors flocked to the cobblestone River Walk anyway, to eat at the sidewalk cafés and tour the historic district on river barges. If a mall were available, they could also buy souvenirs and further improve the economy of San Antonio.

Washington, D.C., was paying attention as Henry Cisneros made headlines across the country. In 1984, Mayor Cisneros was asked to be a speaker at the 1984 Democratic National Convention that was held in San Francisco. In his late night speech, he said:

> We teach our children in this country when they are four or five years old . . . the Pledge of Allegiance, and its closing lines say that we are . . . one Nation, under God, indivisible, with liberty and justice for all. It doesn't say justice for some. It doesn't say justice if you are born in the right neighborhood. It doesn't say justice if you are born with the right last name. It doesn't say justice for you if you are born with a little money. What it says is liberty and justice for all.[1]

Henry Cisneros worked hard to improve the quality of life for all of the residents of San Antonio, rich and poor. He spent a great deal of time out talking to citizens in order to learn about their concerns. As in all cities around the United States, drugs were a common problem in San Antonio. As Mayor Cisneros walked the streets, he asked people their advice on how to save the young people from lives of crime and drugs. They also discussed ways to improve the neighborhoods and the schools.

Mayor Cisneros did not just listen to what people said, though. He got out and rode with the police to see what they faced in their daily lives. He did the same with the firefighters and the ambulance drivers. To get a better idea of what kind of work the sanitation workers had to perform, Cisneros collected garbage with them one day. And he often visited the schools to speak with students about the importance of a good education.

Henry Cisneros was a good example of the power of education. He had spent many years in school, learning about city planning so that he could make that his career. His list of credentials was long and impressive when he made his move into the political arena. The problems that he might have encountered because he was a member of an ethnic minority, faded when people saw evidence of his ability and knowledge.

Because he was so convinced that everyone needed a quality education, Henry Cisneros spent a great deal of time pushing for higher standards in the classroom. During 1984, Texas Governor Mark White established the Governor's Task Force on Education to look into problems in the state's schools. After much study and debate, the committee recommended a list of sweeping

Henry Cisneros collects garbage one day in 1984 to see what problems sanitation workers faced.

changes for Texas schools. Henry Cisneros appeared several times before the Texas legislature to help convince the lawmakers that the changes were necessary.

Some of the things that the legislature eventually approved in the education package, called House Bill 72, included head-start programs for children from low-income families. Those programs would provide educational opportunities for very young, low-income children so that they could enter first grade on an equal footing with their more affluent classmates.

The bill also required that classes be smaller in the lower grades, so that teachers would have more time to devote to each student. The committee found a great deal of difference between rich and poor school districts when it came to the amount of money that each had to spend on education. The legislature said that, in the future, allotment of state money would have to be equalized among all of the districts in Texas.

One of the more controversial moves made by the Texas legislature concerned sports and athletes in the state's public schools. In the past, an athlete was allowed to play team sports even if he or she was failing an academic subject. After the passage of House Bill 72, athletes had to stay out of competition for six weeks if they received an "F" in a subject. In addition, the passing grade was raised from 60 to 70, so that students would have to work even harder in order to pass.

There was a great deal of grumbling heard statewide,

Henry Cisneros gives a speech in support of public libraries.

especially from athletes and their coaches. In spite of the complaints though, the new rules provided some strong incentives for many students, and caused them to try a little harder in school. As a result of the new education bill that Henry Cisneros helped pass, many other changes were also made in an effort to improve the system so that every public school student in Texas could receive a quality education.

Henry and Mary Alice's daughters, Teresa and Mercedes, attended private Catholic schools, just as their parents had. On Sundays, the family attended Mass together and then often visited some of their many relatives who lived in the area. Cisneros still jogged several times a week. It was a habit he had gotten into as a student at A&M. Often the mayor could be seen running through the streets in his neighborhood, sometimes accompanied by his wife and daughters. As he passed, people called out to him and waved. He was a well-known figure around the streets of San Antonio.

As mayor, Cisneros had many official duties to perform that were more fun than work. He rode in parades and participated in charity football games. He opened festivals and put on a sombrero to sing along with a mariachi band on more than one occasion. He escorted foreign dignitaries around his city and pointed out the advantages of living and working in San Antonio. During all of his activities, Henry Cisneros was followed by members of the press. He made headlines all

Henry Cisneros was a popular figure around San Antonio. Here he has stopped to speak to a group of students.

of the time at home, but one particular event in his life made news nationwide.

In 1984, Democratic presidential candidate and former Vice President Walter Mondale, was conducting interviews in his search for a vice-presidential running mate. Thirty-seven-year-old Henry Cisneros was included on his list of possibilities. The Cisneros family was invited to Mondale's home in Minnesota for a meeting. Teresa, age thirteen, and Mercedes, age eight, accompanied their parents on the trip. The Cisneros family spent several hours inside the Mondale home, talking to the former Vice President and his wife.

After the visit, they all went outside on the driveway and answered questions for members of the press who were gathered there. Henry Cisneros related a little of his family history as he said:

> When my grandfather crossed into Texas from Mexico, he could never have imagined that someday one of his own would be interviewed for the vice-presidency of the United States. The fact that this is happening is a testimony to the openness of American society and is proof that if we have faith in people and give them the tools to work with, they will achieve.[2]

Henry Cisneros was not selected to be Walter Mondale's running mate in 1984. Instead Mondale chose Representative Geraldine Ferraro of New York. The Democratic candidate eventually lost the election to the incumbent, President Ronald Reagan. Just to be interviewed for the position was an honor. It once again put Henry Cisneros in the national spotlight and gave the city of San Antonio a little free publicity.

After the trip to Minnesota, Mayor Cisneros returned to the business at hand, the business of improving the economy of his city. San Antonio had already come a long way under the leadership of Cisneros. The poorest neighborhoods in the city had once been training grounds for Peace Corps volunteers who were about to be sent to underdeveloped countries to work. The San Antonio slums, filled with desperately poor people who often lived in shacks, did not look too different from poverty-stricken areas in South America. Thankfully, that reality of San Antonio life was beginning to disappear.

In its place rose a city full of new opportunities for all of its residents. The health-care industry was expanding and a Research Park Foundation was created to help promote the bioscience and health-science research facility. The Rivercenter Mall was more than just an idea, and a major hotel chain announced plans to build a 1,000-room hotel in the area of the proposed mall. A new terminal had to be added to the airport to handle the increased number of visitors who arrived in San Antonio from all over the world. The growth meant jobs for the city's residents and jobs meant a better standard of living.

When it came time for the 1985 elections, there was no question that Henry Cisneros would run for mayor again. He did and won handily with 73 percent of the vote. Discussions had been going on for some time about the possibility of a Sea World amusement park for San Antonio. During Cisneros's third term those talks became reality when access roads were built to enable the park to begin construction. When the park was finished, it would be the biggest Sea World in the United States and a great boon to the tourist industry of San Antonio.

Henry Cisneros was known all over the city and was called by his first name most of the time. His phone number was in the directory and he seemed to be unusually accessible to the public. Henry's parents lived in the same house they owned when he was a child, and he often jogged over to visit with them. Since childhood, they had called their son "Quico" (pronounced Key-ko), which is short for Enrique, the Spanish form of Henry.[3]

As his third term in the mayor's office came to a close, things seemed to be going very well for Henry Cisneros, both politically and personally. The economy of San Antonio continued to improve and many of the Target '90 goals were becoming realities. At home, Mary Alice and Henry looked forward to the birth of their third child, who was due in the early summer of 1987. With three successful terms in office behind him, Henry Cisneros ran for and won a fourth term as mayor, this time with 67 percent of the vote.

Henry Cisneros's campaign poster for the 1985 election.

7

Exit From Politics

His fourth term in office began smoothly as Cisneros continued with his programs of economic growth. He said that "my fundamental objective has been stated forthrightly since I first ran for city council." That objective is "to raise incomes and help reduce the poverty percentage, to help the overall economy grow so that there'll be enough resources to deal with the ethnic unfairness of the past."[1]

The population of San Antonio was 860,000 in 1987, and it was listed as the tenth-largest city in the United States.[2] Henry Cisneros had a lot of people and projects to think about. His days were spent speeding from one activity to another, reading reports, and talking on his car phone when he was away from the office. He often drove by his home to check on the construction work being done there.

The old, two-bedroom house that the Cisneros family lived in was getting too small. Instead of buying a newer and larger house, the family decided to add on to their home and stay where they were. The renovation plans were extensive and several rooms were being added. In the meantime, the family was living in a rented house until the work could be completed, hopefully in time for the new arrival.

On June 10, 1987, John Paul Cisneros was born. The pregnancy and delivery had been difficult for Mary Alice. Shortly after his birth, an examination detected that the baby had a badly deformed heart. Instead of having the normal four chambers and four valves, the baby's heart functioned as if it only had two chambers and three valves. Henry Cisneros later said that John Paul's heart did not even sound like a normal heart. "Most human hearts go ker-thump, ker-thump. His goes swish, swish, swish."[3]

John Paul was also born without a spleen, an organ that helps filter bacteria from the blood and also produces antibodies that help to fight infection. The baby would not only suffer from a congenital heart defect, he would also probably have more infections, and they could be serious because of his weakened immune system. The doctors told Henry and Mary Alice that their newborn son could die immediately or might live

Mercedes, Mary Alice, and Teresa Cisneros look at baby names a few months before the birth of John Paul.

to be five or six, or even older. If he were to live, several major surgeries would have to be performed to try and repair his heart. All his parents could do was take him home and love him.

Shortly after his son was born, Henry Cisneros said:

> The birth of this baby is a different kind of experience. Most of my life has revolved around doing things that you can know and predict what the outcome will be, and everything's done on a deadline. With this there's no solution and no deadline. You have to just keep building him up and hoping that some mildly life-extending procedure will be invented that will buy you some time. You can't engineer a solution. You can't fix it.[4]

Mary Alice and Henry Cisneros took their young son home and tried to lead a normal life with their other two children. Sixteen-year-old Teresa and twelve-year-old Mercedes were grown up enough to help with their tiny baby brother. John Paul had to be fed often because of his small size, and always there was the worry of an infection. The mayor said: "We'll go forward. It's a day-by-day thing. If the test here is to see how much I can carry—well, I can carry it."[5]

As the weeks passed, Mayor Cisneros slowly resumed his duties to the city. There was speculation that he would resign, but he continued on in office. Business had carried on as usual during the temporary absence of the mayor. Pope John Paul II, leader of the Roman

John Paul Cisneros being baptized at Sacred Heart Catholic Church on June 21, 1987.

Catholic Church, was expected to pay a visit to the city in September. (The Cisneros baby had been named after the pope.) Numerous preparations were underway to accommodate the huge crowds that were expected to come to see Pope John Paul. On the day of his appearance, 300,000 people were there to cheer the pontiff as he said Mass and blessed those who were gathered before him.

In 1987 the Census Bureau reported that San Antonio had moved up from the number ten spot to become the ninth-largest city in the country. The acres of suburbs that had grown up around the city were home to thousands of new San Antonio residents. The computer and health-related industries continued to grow and needed more and more employees. Sea World opened in May 1988, and the Rivercenter Mall continued to expand, giving tourists even more reasons to visit San Antonio. Mayor Cisneros also had big plans to build a domed sports stadium in his city so that major entertainment and sports events could be scheduled.

With everything seeming to go according to his plans, Henry Cisneros unexpectedly announced on September 12, 1988, that he would not run for a fifth term in office. He said that personal responsibilities were too great for him to continue as mayor. His son's medical bills were growing and his daughters were almost ready for college. The mayor's salary of $4,000 was far too small for the number of hours that he put

Twenty-month-old John Paul visits his father's office in City Hall.

into the job. To supplement his tiny income, Henry Cisneros had always made extra money by teaching courses at the area colleges. He was also paid for giving speeches to various organizations around the country, but he needed to make more money for his family. He would have to step down and let someone else run San Antonio.

Just a month after his announcement not to seek a fifth term, Henry Cisneros admitted to the media that as rumored, he had been having an extramarital affair for the past two years. During a 45-minute press conference outside of his home he said that "I am a human being, in addition to being mayor. I am not perfect . . . [but] I intend to carry on."[6] Mary Alice Cisneros stayed inside the couple's home during the interview. Later, Mrs. Cisneros said: "I'm not falling apart. I'm not in tears. I'm standing strong in my faith."[7] Soon after the affair was made public, Mary Alice and Henry Cisneros separated for nearly a year. Late in 1989, the couple reconciled. Then, in 1991, Mary Alice Cisneros filed for divorce, but withdrew the suit a short time later.[8]

The Hispanic-American community was losing one of their most visible representatives. Andy Hernandez, a politically active San Antonio resident said: "There's a feeling of loss that Henry wasn't all that people thought he was, and I think the Hispanic electorate will be tougher on one of their own than the rest of the community in the short run."[9]

The scandal seemed to bring an end to the political life of Henry Cisneros. He announced plans to open a business called Cisneros Assets Management Company. It would be a pension-fund management firm that assisted some of the growing number of Hispanic Americans in the United States with their assets. On May 31, 1989, Mayor Cisneros spent his last day in office and on June 1, he became a private citizen again.

For the first time in fourteen years, Henry Cisneros would have some extra time to spend with his family and friends. John Paul was nearly two years old and appeared to be a happy, relatively healthy child. He still had to undergo some major open-heart surgery, but for the time being, he was doing well.

Even though Henry Cisneros was no longer making news as mayor, his name continued to appear in local and state publications. Supporters lined up to praise the work that Cisneros had done for the city. San Antonio City Manager Lou Fox said: "He was a magnificent mayor." City Councilwoman Maria Berriozabal added: "San Antonio is a different city than it was eight years ago. San Antonio needed what Henry brought in '81. We were asleep, and he came to wake us up."[10] Texas Governor Bill Clements added that "Henry has certainly been a leader for San Antonio and, indeed, for our state. His commitment and his tireless efforts have brought new jobs and opportunities to a city that is better for his dedicated service."[11]

Henry Cisneros at his desk on May 31, 1989, his last day in office as mayor of San Antonio, Texas.

Indeed, the efforts of Henry Cisneros had forever changed the face of San Antonio. The city is now home to the third-largest applied research institute in this country. More than 50,000 people are employed in the health-related industry. San Antonio has also become a world-recognized leader in the treatment of serious burn victims. The Rivercenter Mall was completed, along with Sea World and the Alamodome, a 65,000-seat sports arena. Opryland of Nashville built a theme park, called Fiesta Texas, that has the world's tallest and fastest wooden roller coaster. All of the projects were started during the mayoral terms of Henry Cisneros.

The city also has undergone more than $500 million worth of capital improvements that included street repair, freeway construction, and better drainage for those areas of town that used to flood after every rain. New city parks and libraries dot the neighborhoods in and around San Antonio. The city looks and feels more prosperous than it did in the years before Henry Cisneros became mayor.

When asked in 1990 if he would ever run for mayor again, Cisneros replied that "for the first time in a very long time I feel relieved of the burden of governing San Antonio. I can't go back again, even if I wanted to. The momentum is gone."[12] Texans speculated that maybe another public office was out there with Henry Cisneros's name on it, maybe governor of Texas or a cabinet appointment in Washington, D.C.

8

Private Citizen

For the time being, Henry Cisneros would just be a private citizen. No longer did he have to deal with the day-to-day problems that faced the ninth-largest city in the United States. The life of the forty-one-year-old ex-mayor was not empty though. His new company required a great deal of time in the early months. Cisneros and his associates needed to build up their client list if they expected to see their company grow and prosper.

Henry's family also needed his attention. Teresa was seventeen years old and nearly ready to begin college, and her thirteen-year-old sister, Mercedes, was about to start high school. John Paul was two and continued to do well, but he would have to undergo major surgery at some time in the future. The former mayor's extramarital affair also continued to be a topic of discussion in the San Antonio newspapers, even though the woman involved had moved to another city. In 1989, Henry Cisneros had more than enough challenges to keep him occupied.

In addition to his business and family responsibilities, Cisneros continued to be involved in political activities. There were nearly twenty million Hispanic Americans in the United States, and they needed leadership in order to unite and develop an agenda that addressed their problems. Henry Cisneros had recognized the need for unity and helped form the National Hispanic Leadership Agenda (NHLA) in 1987. Hispanic-American leaders from all across the country made up the membership of the organization.

Because all Hispanic Americans do not share a common country of origin, many different groups had formed over the years. Puerto Rican immigrants to the United States had one organization, and former Cuban residents another, while Mexican Americans belonged to yet other groups. One of the oldest Hispanic-American organizations in America was the League of United Latin American Citizens (LULAC), which was established in 1929. Its more than 100,000 members were active in seeking economic, political, and educational equality for Hispanics.

Another established group was the National Council of La Raza, which was founded in 1968. Its members were advocates of equal civil rights for Hispanics. The NHLA sought to join all Hispanic people and groups together and address their common concerns. Henry Cisneros said that the mission of the organization was to "provide Hispanic America with a clear, central voice, and thereby a more powerful impact on issues of civic and public policy."[1]

In 1960, when Henry Cisneros was thirteen years old, only about seven million Hispanic Americans lived in the United States. Just thirty years later, the number had risen to nearly 22.4 million. During the ten years between 1980 and 1990, the Hispanic-American population in the United States increased more than 53 percent. By comparison, the white population grew by only 6 percent and the African-American by 13.2 percent.[2] By 2020, it was projected that Hispanic Americans would be the largest minority group in the country. Even though their numbers continued to climb, their political clout remained small. A 1991 report, by the National Association of Latino Elected Officials, found that Hispanic-American politicians made up only 1 percent of elected officials.[3]

It was difficult to get Hispanic-American politicians elected because Hispanic-American voters turned out in such small numbers at the polls. In Houston, Texas, alone, 45.8 percent of Hispanics who were old enough to vote could not go to the polls on election day because they were not citizens of the United States.[4] On a nationwide scale, millions of Hispanics were barred from voting because they had not become citizens. Those who were citizens often did not vote either, sometimes because of a lack of interest. Others stayed away from the polls because of a lack of knowledge about the candidates and issues and an inability to read and understand the English language.

In order to get more Hispanic Americans involved in the political process, better information needed to be made available to them about the naturalization procedures. Many more Hispanic Americans might become United States citizens if they understood the rules better and felt less intimidated by them. In addition, awareness and interest in the political candidates and the issues needed to be encouraged through education.

There again though, Hispanic Americans were at a disadvantage. According to a study done in 1991, they had the highest school dropout rate in the country. An American Council of Education report found that only 51 percent of Hispanic-American students completed high school.[5] A lack of education often seems to go hand in hand with a life of poverty.

In 1990, 28 percent of Hispanic Americans in the United States lived below the poverty level.[6] Many of them depended on public assistance to help pay for food and rent. There was a definite need for education and training to enable those people to get better jobs and earn more money for their families. Maybe the NHLA would be able to draw attention to some of the problems that Hispanic Americans faced in their everyday lives.

Henry Cisneros was not just interested in the futures of Hispanic Americans. He also continued to be interested in all the people of his city. He often visited the local schools to give pep talks to the students about the importance of a good education. He encouraged students to learn about computers and the technologies of the future. He also appeared on numerous television programs and gave speeches to various civic and business organizations. Even though he was no longer a public servant, he remained in the public eye.

Other public figures that Henry Cisneros would come to know well were then Arkansas Governor Bill Clinton and Tennessee Senator Al Gore. The 1992 presidential elections were approaching, and Clinton and Gore were chosen by the Democratic party to be their candidates for the country's highest offices. Henry Cisneros was also a member of the Democratic party, as well as an experienced politician. Perhaps the Clinton campaign could use his talents during the months before the election. Cisneros might also be able to attract some of the Hispanic-American vote to the Democratic ticket.

Henry Cisneros did join the Clinton team and was soon named as a senior advisor to the campaign. Throughout the summer and fall of 1992, Cisneros and hundreds of other Democrats traveled around the

Henry Cisneros shows the Japanese ambassador around the University of Texas Institute of Texan Cultures in San Antonio.

United States in support of the Clinton-Gore ticket. They attended hundreds of rallies, where they gave speeches and shook hands. They tried to convince the voters that Bill Clinton was the best person for the job in Washington. When the long and tiring campaign finally wound down in the fall of 1992, the weary Clinton crusaders returned home and left the outcome of the election in the hands of the voters.

On November 3, 1992, only 54 percent of America's 189,000,000 registered voters made a trip to the polls to cast their ballots. When the numbers were all tallied and the electoral college votes cast, Bill Clinton was declared to be the winner of the election. The Democratic candidate had received 43 percent of the votes cast. Incumbent President George Bush was denied a second term in office having only amassed a 38 percent vote total. Independent candidate Ross Perot came in third, with a 19 percent share.[7] Bill Clinton was elected to be the forty-second President of the United States.

Henry Cisneros had done a good job during the Clinton campaign. He was back in the political arena and appeared to be right at home. When he decided not to run for a fifth term as mayor of San Antonio, and admitted to having an extramarital affair, many thought his political career was over. Now, after the successful Clinton campaign, the skeptics were not so sure. Shortly after the election and before the inauguration, Bill Clinton began to select his advisors and cabinet members. Would Henry Cisneros be selected to fill a spot in the new administration?

On December 7, 1992, President-elect Bill Clinton nominated Henry Cisneros to be secretary of the Department of Housing and Urban Development (HUD). Also present at the announcement in Little Rock, Arkansas, were Henry Cisneros's wife Mary Alice, and the couple's three children. Teresa was now twenty-one years old and a college student. Mercedes was seventeen and a high school senior, and John Paul, age five, was a relatively healthy child who had not yet started school.

They were not the only family members who proudly watched as Henry Cisneros became the first Hispanic American to be nominated to the Clinton cabinet. At home in San Antonio were Henry's parents, Elvira and George Cisneros. They were gathered around the television set with some of their family and friends, to watch their "Quico" be nominated for a Cabinet level post.

Henry Cisneros seemed to be right back where he belonged, in the world of politics and public service. After the nomination was announced, the forty-five-year-old Cisneros was described by one of his advisors as "the happiest man in America. It's like a great burden has been lifted from him."[8] It seemed that Henry Cisneros had managed successfully to overcome his past difficulties and make a political comeback on a grand scale.

In addition to his public success, the private life of Cisneros had also taken a turn for the better. Mary Alice said: "Henry and I have put our problems behind us. What is past is past. We're getting on with our lives."[9] It looked as if a move to Washington would be in the Cisneros family's future. But first, there would be a confirmation hearing to determine if Henry Cisneros was the appropriate man for the HUD job.

9

Housing and Urban Development

The U.S. Senate Committee on Banking, Housing and Urban Affairs convened on January 12, 1993. The members of the committee gathered to question Henry Cisneros about his views concerning the mounting problems that faced public housing and the cities. They would decide whether or not Bill Clinton's nominee was acceptable for the position of secretary of the Department of Housing and Urban Development. If their vote was favorable, the nomination of Henry Cisneros would then be passed on for a full Senate vote.

During the first part of the proceedings, the two senators from Cisneros's home state of Texas spoke out in support of the nominee. Senator Lloyd Bentsen, who was about to be confirmed as the new secretary of the Treasury, said about Henry Cisneros: "He is recognized as one of our nation's most innovative mayors."¹ Senator Phil Gramm related that he had known the nominee since Cisneros was a student at A&M, while Gramm was a professor there. He said: "Henry was a smart, dedicated student. He was respected by his professors and his peers. He was a student leader, he was active in the Corps, he was a model student at Texas A&M."²

After additional words of praise were heard from Bentsen, Gramm, and several others, the hearing moved on to discussion of the serious issues that faced HUD in the 1990s. The problems in many of America's inner cities had reached a critical point. Gun battles raged as gangs and drug dealers terrorized the residents of dilapidated housing projects. Homeless people slept in doorways, and poverty and hunger were becoming an all-too-common sight. Public housing projects were no longer a safe place for the poor to live. They had become warehouses full of frightened people who were quickly losing hope in the American dream.

In 1991, 35.7 million people in the United States were living below the poverty level. That amounted to more than 14 percent of the population of this country.³ What was even more alarming, 40 percent of those living in poverty were children.⁴ During his confirmation hearings, Henry Cisneros had expressed concern that "an entire generation of our young people is slipping away." He then went on to say: "More and more, the people of our country seem to be divided by race, intimidated by crime, and isolated from the economic mainstream."[5]

Cisneros expressed an interest in joining with some of the other social welfare agencies in order to coordinate services.[6] Poor people needed more than just shelter to enable them to escape from the cycle of poverty. They desperately needed to learn job skills that would allow them to become self-sufficient. They also needed counseling to help them make the correct choices about child care and health issues such as pregnancy and nutrition. Henry Cisneros was well known in San Antonio for his skill in getting different groups to work together for the common good. Maybe he would also have an opportunity to try his magic at the national level.

After meeting for only four hours, the Senate Committee on Banking, Housing and Urban Affairs recessed the hearing. The committee members had a few days to consider all that they had heard from and about Henry Cisneros, and then a final vote would be taken on the matter. On January 19, 1993, the committee members voted and agreed to pass the nomination of Cisneros on to the full Senate. On January 21, 1993, the Senate approved the appointment, and Henry Cisneros became the new secretary of Housing and Urban Development. His new job would include a careful examination of the problems that faced public housing in America. The history of public housing could be

Henry Cisneros shortly after his appointment as secretary of Housing and Urban Development.

traced back to some of the most difficult days in our nation's past.

Beginning in 1929, the United States experienced more than a decade of what would later be called the Great Depression. The stock market crash on October 29, 1929, started a downward spiral in the American economy. Over the following months and years, hundreds of banks failed in large cities and small towns all across the country. Thousands of people lost whatever money they had deposited in those banks. The value of stocks also began to plunge, until many large and small companies ran out of money and closed their doors.

Unemployment figures rose higher and higher, from 1.5 million to 3.2 million in just the five months after Black Tuesday.[7] Many families ran out of money and could no longer make the payments on their houses and apartments. The lucky ones were able to move in with friends or family members. Many others had nowhere to go and found shelter where they could.

It was not until 1933, after President Franklin D. Roosevelt took office, that changes began to take place. At that time, one-fourth of the work force in America was unemployed. Five thousand banks had collapsed, taking with them the over nine million savings accounts. The income of the country was only one-half of what it had been in 1930.[8] Almost immediately, President

Roosevelt initiated government projects that were designed to put as many people back to work as possible.

In order to employ thousands of people, a massive building effort was begun. Over the next few years, the government funded projects that included the construction of new roads, schools, and parks. As Roosevelt's first term drew to a close, the unemployment figures were lower, but there were still millions of people who were unable to afford decent housing.

During Roosevelt's re-election campaign of 1936, he said:

> We have spent large sums of money on parks, on highways, on bridges, on museums, and for other projects of civic betterment. But we have not yet begun adequately to spend money in order to help the families in the overcrowded sections of our cities to live as citizens have a right to live.[9]

Soon after Roosevelt was re-elected to a second term, he signed into law a bill that created the United States Housing Authority. It established a program that was designed to provide government-subsidized housing to low-income tenants. During the next few years, federally funded homes and apartments were built throughout the nation, usually in urban areas. The construction of additional public housing was temporarily halted after the outbreak of World War II. At that time, it was necessary to concentrate the resources of the nation in the defense industries.

When the country geared up to produce the weapons and vehicles needed for the war, the economy quickly improved. With so many men overseas fighting the war, thousands of women went to work for the first time. Unemployment figures plunged and prosperity returned to the country. Once the war ended, however, thousands of soldiers returned to their families. Many had gotten married and needed homes of their own. Some could afford to pay for housing, but there were still many who needed assistance. In order to help those who were still in need, low-income housing assistance was offered again and has been available ever since.

Through the years, the type of tenants in public housing projects gradually changed. During the early years of government-subsidized housing, most of the people who lived in the projects were able to contribute some money toward the payment of their rent. Very few depended entirely on the government for all of their needs. But almost fifty years later, when Henry Cisneros was named secretary of HUD, the picture was dramatically different.

In 1992, the average income for families who lived in public housing was only $7,394.[10] Many of the residents were single mothers with several children. Nearly everyone in the "projects" depended heavily on government assistance not only for housing, but also for other necessities such as food.

The welfare recipients needed much more than just a roof over their heads. They needed education and job training, as well as child care and counseling. Perhaps the new director of HUD would be able to bring some of the government agencies together to work on the problems of poverty in America. Henry Cisneros certainly had an enormous task in front of him as he began his work at HUD.

10

Sorting Out the Problems at HUD

Early in 1993, Henry Cisneros moved his personal belongings into the large, tenth-floor office at the HUD headquarters in Washington, D.C. He then spent some time getting to know many of the 3,750 employees who worked there. As he walked through the halls meeting people, he asked some HUD staffers questions about their jobs and what part they played in the department. As the weeks passed, Henry Cisneros began to examine the giant task of overseeing HUD.

The more than 3,000 HUD employees in Washington, D.C., were just part of the 13,555 people who worked for HUD nationwide. Overall, HUD supervised nearly one and a half million individual housing units that were occupied by over three million tenants.[1] A small army of people was employed to look after the buildings and keep track of the people who lived in them.

During his first months in office, Secretary Cisneros said that he wanted to "reinvent HUD." He intended to try and make the rules and regulations less confusing. He also wanted to publish clearer information about HUD programs so that they could be better understood.[2] As mayor of San Antonio, Henry Cisneros had been able to sort through many of the HUD rules, and he helped obtain a total of $230 million in government money for his city. He often used government money to help persuade private enterprise to build in San Antonio. Private investors were more likely to start projects if they could be guaranteed a certain amount of federal assistance.

For example, the Rivercenter Mall was built with $19 million in public or government money, but private investors spent more than $200 million on the project.[3] As secretary of HUD, perhaps Henry Cisneros would once again be able to get government and the private sector to cooperate. Before he made an attempt to ask other agencies for help though, he needed to straighten out the image problem that plagued HUD.

During the previous few years, one scandal after another had rocked the department. Several HUD officials were indicted for such offenses as mail fraud, bribery, and influence peddling. Billions of dollars that were supposed to go to help the poor were instead lost due to fraud, poor management, and bureaucratic bungling. Jack Kemp, the secretary of HUD just before Cisneros, was successful in getting a number of reforms enacted. He tried to get the agency's reputation cleaned up, but his term of office ended before the job was completed. Henry Cisneros would have to take over and try to finish what Jack Kemp had started. He could add that job to his ever-growing list of duties.

After only a short time in office, Cisneros was asked about his new job. He said:

> I concluded that if I was going to sell my business, move the family up here, put myself back into public life again, then the only reason to do it is to do something that I really care about. For me, that agenda is helping the poorest of the poor, making communities livable, and doing all within my power to avoid more pain in inner cities.[4]

It did not take Henry Cisneros long to identify some of the most serious problems that his agency had to deal with. In a speech to the National Press Club in April 1993, Cisneros said: "Large public housing developments have concentrated the poorest of the poor in housing that is overly dense, poorly designed, badly built, and located in isolated, segregated neighborhoods."[5] Actually, the federal government itself was responsible for the problems in many of the public housing projects.

During the 1950s and 1960s the government

decided to move away from what was called low-rise public housing. The low-rise projects were groups of apartments that were no more than two stories tall and were spread out over a fairly large area. Instead, high-rise developments were built in large cities all over America. The multistory buildings seemed like a good idea at the time. They did not take up much space and they could house thousands of poor people in one, central location. They were not luxury apartments, but they were nice and they were new. Problems arose because the projects did not stay nice and new for long and, as they deteriorated, they attracted less desirable tenants who were often socially irresponsible.

The Robert Taylor Homes in Chicago is a good example of a high-rise project. When it was built, it consisted of twenty-eight identical buildings of sixteen floors each, with about ten apartments per floor. The project was crammed into a one-half mile by two mile area that had little in the way of grass or trees.[6] Because the multistory building's elevators were often out of order, residents on the upper floors often had to either walk up and down many flights of stairs or stay at home.

Even when the elevators were working, it was very difficult for mothers to watch their children play outside. Their apartments were several floors up and they could not get downstairs quickly. Because there were not many safe places for children to play, they often gathered in the halls and on the stairs, instead of outside in the fresh air.

There were projects like Robert Taylor Homes scattered all over the inner cities. Instead of solving the housing problem, they created a whole new set of worries. The run-down buildings became havens for welfare cheats, drug dealers, and gang members. Thugs could easily hide among the maze of stairwells and alleyways and transact their illegal business deals. Gunfire became an all too common sound.

It was eventually apparent that high-rise apartment housing for the poor was a bad idea, and no more multistory apartment buildings were built after 1970. But, many of those original high-rise housing projects were still in use in America's largest cities. Over the years, they had become even older and more dilapidated, and maintenance costs for the run-down buildings were staggering. It was the high cost of construction and maintenance that led the federal government to develop the voucher system as an alternative means of public housing assistance.

In the voucher program, low-income tenants could rent apartments anywhere in town from private owners. The tenants were asked to contribute what they could to help pay part of the monthly rent. The government then paid the landlord the rest of the rent in the form of a voucher. This program allowed Washington, D.C., to stay out of the construction and maintenance business, but still provided assistance to poor people.

The voucher program also helped spread low-income, less-educated residents around the city, so that they were not concentrated in just one location. The poor tenants could live among working people who had jobs and were able to support their families with little or no assistance from the government. Sometimes two or three generations of a welfare family had been trapped in a cycle of poverty. Years of public assistance had robbed them of the desire to improve their lives and escape from the welfare system. By living among people who had jobs and supported themselves, some welfare recipients saw the advantages in ending their dependence on government handouts. In the high-rise projects, so few people worked that there were no role models for the welfare recipients to emulate.

It took a long time for the problems of the high-rise apartments to become apparent. Once their very serious shortcomings were realized, smaller complexes were again constructed that were similar to the ones built before the high-rise concept. The newer projects were usually not built in the inner city, but were constructed in or around suburban neighborhoods. Efforts were also made to see that the housing was more livable, and grassy areas were included so that children could safely play outside.

One such low-rise housing project in Vidor, Texas, became the scene of a confrontation between Henry

Cisneros and some of the local residents of the town. Vidor, a town of 11,000 located 100 miles east of Houston, had a long history of racial intolerance. There were few if any African-American residents in the town and the Ku Klux Klan (KKK) had held several rallies there in the recent past. The KKK is a white supremacist organization that traces its roots to the time of the Civil War in America. There was also a forty-year-old, seventy-four unit public housing project in town, called the Vidor Villa.

The Orange County Housing Authority, the government bureau that ran the project, was given an ultimatum in 1991 by HUD officials. An order was issued to desegregate the units or lose government funding. The Civil Rights Act of 1964 prohibited discrimination in employment, in public housing, or in programs that received federal funds. Since the Department of Housing and Urban Development ". . . is charged with ensuring fair housing opportunities and combating discrimination against home buyers . . .",[7] Vidor Villa would have to comply with the law.

Four African-American adults were moved into the complex in 1993, but all of them soon moved out after being threatened and taunted with racial slurs. No other African Americans could be found who were willing to move into the apartments. The situation got so bad that Henry Cisneros himself went to the town in September 1993, and seized control of Vidor Villa. The housing project would be operated by HUD until the desegregation problems could be overcome.

When Henry Cisneros visited Vidor in September, he spoke before a cheering crowd that was gathered at the local Catholic Church. He said: "The United States Government cannot stand by when federal money is involved and hear stories about people being afraid to move where they want to."[8] He later said about the incident in Vidor: "We don't, in America in 1993, anywhere tell anyone they can't live anywhere because of the color of their skin."[9]

In an attempt to desegregate the project, HUD officials began trying to find African Americans who were willing to move into the apartments. The search was prolonged, because few African-American families wanted to risk living in the town. While HUD personnel interviewed prospective tenants, the volatile situation at Vidor Villa gradually settled down. Only time would tell what the final outcome of the HUD takeover would be.

Back in Washington, Henry Cisneros had just a few months left of his first year as secretary of the Department of Housing and Urban Development. He was more familiar with the problems in the agency and was in the process of formulating his goals for 1994. At home, the Cisneros family was growing accustomed to living in Washington, D.C., and had recently experienced a very important event in their lives.

11

Solutions

Earlier in the summer of 1993, a long-awaited decision was made by the doctors who cared for John Paul Cisneros. The physicians decided that it was time to operate on the child and try to reshape his badly deformed heart. The very serious open-heart surgery was scheduled for July. Henry Cisneros said: "I couldn't bear his questions. Nothing in my life has prepared me for this. Nothing could rival the sense of total panic that comes over me when I think of this surgery."[1]

John Paul was admitted to the Children's Hospital of Philadelphia early in July, to prepare for the surgery. When the day finally arrived, the boy was wheeled into the operating room, while his parents waited for the doctor to reappear. After a two-and-a-half-hour operation, the chief of cardiovascular surgery emerged to tell Henry and Mary Alice Cisneros that the surgery had gone very well. Doctor William Norwood said that the restructuring "created a four-chambered heart that effectively performed the functions of a normal heart."[2]

John Paul remained in the hospital for a couple of weeks after the operation, so that the doctors could carefully monitor the activity of his heart. He recovered quickly and his parents were told to expect a normal life span for their son. After all the years of uncertainty, Mary Alice and Henry Cisneros could finally look forward to their son's future. In September, John Paul started kindergarten. The first day of school was more than just the beginning of his education. For John Paul, it was also the start of a new, healthy life.

With the successful surgery behind them, the Cisneros family could once again concentrate on their other duties. Unfortunately, none of the difficulties that HUD had to deal with had magically gone away during the summer of 1993. Tension continued to build in the inner cities because people who were too poor were crowded into housing projects that were too small. Gangs ruled the terrain in many areas and the homeless population continued to increase. When he was faced with the seemingly insurmountable situation, Henry Cisneros did what had worked for him in the past.

When he became mayor of San Antonio in 1981, Henry Cisneros had a vision for the city that he was to govern. His hard work, along with the efforts of many volunteers, led to the development of the "Target '90" program. It proved to be a good set of goals to work by and eventually led to the economic rebirth of San Antonio. Because "Target '90" was successful, Cisneros also developed a vision for HUD, and issued a forty-three-point plan he called "Creating Windows of Opportunity." His six priorities would be to reduce homelessness, renovate deteriorated public housing, provide more affordable housing, open up housing to minorities, support neighborhood economic development, and improve HUD management.[3]

He unveiled his plan in an address to about fifteen hundred employees in the HUD cafeteria. He issued a "call to action" to help solve the problems of the poor and the cities. The increasing numbers of homeless people in America was one of the issues that needed immediate attention. Latest figures put the homeless population somewhere between six hundred thousand and three million.[4]

One plan that had the potential to help the homeless had been approved during the summer. HUD and the Department of Health and Human Services (HHS) agreed to provide nearly $17 million for a five-year trial project called ACCESS. The money would be spent to take care of homeless people who had severe mental illnesses as well as addictions to drugs and alcohol. It is estimated that up to one-third of all homeless people

As mayor of San Antonio, Henry Cisneros worked hard to improve the city with his "Target 90" goals.

suffer from mental illnesses such as schizophrenia or manic-depressive disorder.[5]

Some people in America had come to fear the homeless. Beggars were becoming more and more aggressive as they panhandled. Alcoholics and drug addicts slept on the sidewalks and in the doorways of many buildings. The sight of homeless people had become so common that some in America began to resent and fear their growing numbers. Henry Cisneros said: "A backlash is growing. What I believed was an almost universal compassion has today given way to an impatience, a frustration, an anger toward the homeless."[6]

In San Francisco, seats in the bus shelters were being redesigned so that people could not sleep comfortably on them. In Madison, Wisconsin, "aggressive panhandling" was outlawed. And all across the nation, donations to food banks had fallen off ". . . by as much as 40% this Thanksgiving."[7] No longer were many of the homeless people looked upon with sympathy. Instead, they were viewed by some as another frightening aspect of our already frightening society. Something had to be done quickly to help solve the problem, and ACCESS was one program that was being tested.

Mental health agencies everywhere were eligible to apply for ACCESS funds and to participate in the program. HUD and the Department of Health and Human Services joined with the Departments of

Education, Veterans Affairs, Labor, and Agriculture to develop ACCESS. During his mayoral days, Henry Cisneros had great success when he brought different groups together to work as a team. It was beginning to look like he could make cooperation between the agencies work on the national level also.

Only a few days before Christmas 1993, the homeless crisis came particularly close to Henry Cisneros and the employees at HUD. Just across from their office, a homeless woman was found dead after she spent a very cold night in the open. In a response to the tragic event, Cisneros announced that federal buildings would be opened up to house street people during cold weather periods. He also said that his agency would allocate $25 million to help other cities increase their homeless shelters.[8]

A short time after the $25 million HUD announcement, the Clinton administration earmarked $411 million to help the states with their homeless programs. Henry Cisneros said: "There's been kind of an unspoken effort to hide the problem as if it didn't exist. But the problem is so large in our society that we simply can't hide it."[9]

Henry Cisneros had the very difficult task of allocating HUD funds where he thought they were needed most. Even though the department's more than $35 billion budget seemed immense, there were hard decisions to be made about how to spend the money.

Bruce Reed, the deputy assistant to President Clinton for domestic policy, said: "This country has spent billions and billions over the last 30 years on urban America with relatively little impact."[10] New methods would have to be tried in the fight to save the cities and the people within those cities.

After a year at HUD, Cisneros was better able to make the decisions about where the money was needed most. In addition to allocating funds, he also wanted to make the department more efficient so that none of the $35 billion would be wasted. As he looked ahead to 1994, a new opportunity arose for Henry Cisneros, one that had the potential to take him away from Washington, D.C., and back to Texas.

12

The Future?

When Democratic Senator Lloyd Bentsen of Texas was selected by Bill Clinton to be his secretary of the Treasury, Bentsen left behind a vacant U.S. Senate seat. An election was held to fill the rest of Bentsen's term, and a Republican, Kay Bailey Hutchison, won the race by defeating her Democratic opponent. The other Texas Senator, Phil Gramm, was also a Republican.

When it came time for the 1994 election, Henry Cisneros was discussed as a possible Democratic candidate to run against Senator Hutchison. He was well known and respected in Texas, and many felt that he could win the Senate seat back for the Democratic party. Even though Cisneros said that he wanted to remain at HUD, there were many who tried to persuade him to enter the Senate race.

Early in December 1993, Henry Cisneros said: "I have no intention to run for the Senate. I think it would be essentially abandoning my post if I were to walk away."¹ But pressure continued to mount. Hispanic-American groups were especially eager to see Cisneros become a senator so that they would have another representative in Washington. Once again, Cisneros said that he had decided to "absolutely, finally, unequivocally not leave his post as Secretary of HUD."²

His family had just moved into a permanent home in Washington. John Paul was settled in his kindergarten class and was doing well. Teresa was a recent Yale graduate and Mercedes had started college at Stanford University. It just did not seem like the time to get involved in a long and difficult Senate campaign. Cisneros said: "I'm confident enough about my place in life to believe that if I do a good job here, the future will take care of itself."³

In the end, his supporters finally had to believe that Henry Cisneros really meant no. The deadline for filing to run for the Senate seat passed and Cisneros remained at HUD, to continue the work that he started during his first year. His new budget for 1994 included nearly a million dollars more than the 1993 budget.

Some of the almost $36 billion would go to finish up what Henry Cisneros had started at the Vidor Villa a few months earlier. HUD allocated $2.1 million to make improvements to the complex that included a laundry room, air conditioning, and 24-hour security guards and their metal guard house. In addition, HUD would arrange for job training and van transportation for the residents. Eight African-American families had been found to move into Vidor Villa. When they arrived at the apartments, they were accompanied by federal guards who escorted them wherever they wanted to go, inside and outside of the complex.[4]

Some of the new residents were surprised to get smiles, instead of racial taunts from a few of the tenants at Vidor Villa. Many of the African Americans were wary of moving into the previously segregated project, but were determined to do so. One of them said: "I made up my mind from the beginning I was coming, regardless of what had happened, because somebody just has to. You just got to fight for what's right."[5]

As it turned out, the new occupants did not have to fight. Instead they were able to go about their daily lives and become accustomed to their new homes. The eight-foot-tall wire fence that encircled the project and the new rules about visitors, made Vidor Villa a safer place to live. A safe environment was not a description that could be used to describe many other public housing projects. Most resembled war zones, complete with the sounds of gunfire at all hours of the day and night. The Robert Taylor Homes housing project in Chicago recorded 300 reports of gunfire in a five-day period in March 1994.[6]

With the issue of security in mind, Vice President Al Gore announced in February 1994, a plan called "Operation Safe Home." The program was designed to help fight crime in the nation's public housing projects. Gore said that the plan was a display of extraordinary cooperation among various government agencies that included the departments of HUD, Justice, and Treasury. Henry Cisneros said of the plan: "Our message to those who would defraud taxpayers and prey on public housing residents for illegal gain is straightforward and simple. Don't even think about it." Cisneros added that he supported the idea of gun buyouts and prohibiting dealers from selling guns in the projects.[7]

With this and other programs underway, Henry Cisneros continued to search for ways to end some of the misery suffered by the poorest and least productive people in the United States. Ironically, as Cisneros examined the problems of the nation a report was issued concerning his own hometown, San Antonio.

According to a November 1993 study, San Antonio was named as the city with the highest rate of substandard housing of the forty-four U.S. cities that were examined. Thirty-nine percent of its low-income housing was deficient in some major area such as plumbing or heating.[8] Henry Cisneros responded to the statistics by saying: "One of my regrets is that I didn't spend enough time on housing [as mayor]."[9] As secretary of HUD, Cisneros would have ample opportunity to address the housing crisis that faced not only San Antonio, but many other cities as well.

An especially critical housing shortage developed in California early in 1994, when a 6.6 magnitude earthquake struck the Los Angeles area. As many as 15,000 people were left without shelter. Henry Cisneros was sent from Washington, D.C., to survey the damage and oversee some of the disaster relief efforts. The National Guard built tent cities to serve as temporary shelters for the displaced Californians, and emergency HUD certificates were issued to enable many to rent alternative housing. Cisneros visited many of the relief shelters. He talked to some of the earthquake victims in both English and Spanish to make sure that they understood all of their options. When the situation had settled down somewhat, Henry Cisneros returned to Washington, D.C., to resume his work at HUD.

In the spring of 1994, Henry Cisneros spent the night in the Robert Taylor Homes project in Chicago. He talked to the residents and learned of their fears of gangs, guns, and violence. Later, in a speech he said: "In the landscape of urban misery in 1994, Robert Taylor Homes is ground zero." He continued: "The families at Robert Taylor Homes want the same things you and I want: They want to earn a living; they want decent, affordable housing; they want good schools for their children."[10]

In order to make the project safer and more livable,

the government plans to tighten security in the area and promote tenant patrols. In addition, the playgrounds will be cleaned up and programs started for the area's children. Also, vacant apartments that are used by gangs and drug dealers will be renovated and rented to families. Robert Taylor Homes is just one project among hundreds in the United States. Each one has its own unique problems that demand attention from the secretary of HUD.

His job is enormous, but Henry Cisneros seems to be able to face the task. He keeps in good physical condition by carefully watching his diet and jogging several days a week. He said in a recent interview: "I meet kids in housing projects, and they're all firm and tough, and the last thing they want is some pudgy old guy telling them how the world is."[11]

Neither pudgy nor old, Henry Cisneros also credits his apparent good health on a peaceful family life. His twenty-four year marriage to Mary Alice is intact after some bumpy years, and his daughters and six-year-old son are doing well. Cisneros has said: "Anytime you are lightened emotionally you walk a little lighter and smile a little more, and that makes all the difference."[12]

Hopefully, Henry Cisneros will also be able to make a difference in his role as secretary of HUD. If America is to survive, her cities and her poor people must be rehabilitated. When Bill Clinton campaigned for the 1992 presidential election, he pledged to "end welfare as

Henry Cisneros plays football for a charity event. He keeps in good physical shape.

we know it," and promised to find ways for people who depend on public assistance to go to work.[13]

Maybe Henry Cisneros will be instrumental in helping to bring about that change. After only a few weeks on the job, Cisneros recognized a major problem in the agency when he said: "There's a total lack of coordination between HUD and other federal agencies."[14] True to his nature, he quickly established contact with a number of those agencies and the results were programs such as ACCESS and Operation Safe Home.

Maybe future joint ventures among other government departments will result in the formation of additional programs that will help to educate and empower some of the poorest and most dependent people in America. The amazing growth and development of San Antonio, under the direction of Henry Cisneros, is testimony that cooperation among all of the people is one of the surest roads to success.

Chronology

1947—Henry Gabriel Cisneros born in San Antonio, Texas.

1964—Begins college at Texas A&M University.

1968—Receives bachelor's degree from Texas A&M in Urban and Regional Planning.

1969—Marries Mary Alice Perez; named assistant director of Department of Model Cities Program, San Antonio.

1970—Receives master's degree from Texas A&M in Urban and Regional Planning; begins doctoral studies at George Washington University; hired as assistant to executive vice-president of National League of Cities in Washington, D.C.

1971—Named White House Fellow and assistant to Secretary of Health, Education and Welfare Elliott Richardson; daughter Teresa is born.

1972—Enters John F. Kennedy School of Government, at Harvard University in Cambridge, Massachusetts.

1973—Receives master's degree from Harvard University.

1974—Returns to San Antonio as assistant professor at the University of Texas at San Antonio.

1975—Receives doctorate in Public Administration from George Washington University; elected to first term on San Antonio City Council; council member until 1981; daughter Mercedes is born.

1976—Named as one of five Outstanding Young Texans by the Texas Jaycees.

1981—Elected mayor of San Antonio at age 33 with 67 percent of the vote.

1982—Named as one of ten Outstanding Young Men of America by the U.S. Jaycees.

1983—Re-elected to second term as mayor with 94.2 percent of the vote.

1984—Speaker at Democratic National Convention; interviewed by Walter Mondale for vice-presidential spot on Democratic ticket.

1985—Re-elected to third term as mayor with 73 percent of the vote.

1987—Re-elected to fourth term as mayor with 67 percent of the vote; son John Paul born on June 10.

1988—Announces on September 12 he will not run for mayor again.

1989—May 31 is last day as mayor of San Antonio; begins Cisneros Assets Management Company.

1992—On December 17 nominated to become secretary of Housing and Urban Development; nomination confirmed.

1993—On January 22 is sworn into office by Chief Justice William Rehnquist; John Paul Cisneros's heart surgery is successful.

Chapter Notes

Chapter 1

1. Jeffrey Katz, "Domestic Battles," *Congressional Quarterly*, December 11, 1993, p. 154.

2. Bruce Davidson, "Ex-Mayor Nominated to HUD Post," *San Antonio Light*, December 18, 1992, p. A1.

3. United States Senate Committee on Banking and Urban Affairs, Transcript of Confirmation Hearing of Henry Cisneros, January 13, 1993, p. 14.

4. Ibid., p. 113.

Chapter 2

1. Enedelia Obregon, "It's All In the Family," *San Antonio Light*, December 8, 1982, p. D3.

2. John Gillies, *Señor Alcalde* (Minneapolis: Dillon Press, 1988), p. 15.

3. Obregon, p. D3.

4. Linda Chavez, *Out of the Barrio* (New York: HarperCollins, 1991), p. 4.

Chapter 3

1. Stephen Harrigan, "The Time of His Life," *Texas Monthly*, September 1987, p. 136.

2. Kemper Diehl and Jan Jarboe, *Cisneros: Portrait of a New American* (San Antonio, Tex.: Corona Publishing Company, 1985), p. 33.

3. Nicholas Lemann, "First Hispanic," *Esquire*, December 1984, p. 484.

4. Diehl and Jarboe, p. 37.

5. Ibid., p. 34.

6. "Voices From Henry's Past," *San Antonio Light Magazine*, May 3, 1981, p. 9.

7. John W. Kirshon, ed., *Chronicle of America* (New York: Chronicle Publications), p. 802.

8. Diehl and Jarboe, p. 41.

Chapter 4

1. Kemper Diehl and Jan Jarboe, *Cisneros: Portrait of a New American* (San Antonio, Tex.: Corona Publishing Company, 1985), p. 45.

2. "Voices From Henry's Past," *San Antonio Light Magazine*, May 3, 1981, p. 9.

3. Henry Cisneros, "San Antonio: Laying the Foundation For the Future," *USA Today* (magazine), July 1987, p. 25.

4. Diehl and Jarboe, p. 141.

Chapter 5

1. "Now Is the Time Compadres," *Time*, April 13, 1981, p. 59.

2. James McCrory, "Henry Cisneros: The Politician of the Year," *San Antonio Express-News*, December 27, 1981, p. H5.

3. T. R. Fehrenbach, *Lone Star* (New York: Collier Books, 1968), p. 601.

4. George E. Jones, "Take the Initiative," *U.S. News and World Report*, November 23, 1981, p. 65.

5. Nicholas Lemann, "First Hispanic," *Esquire*, December 1984, p. 482.

6. Henry Cisneros, "San Antonio: Laying the Foundation For the Future," *USA Today*, July 1987, p. 33.

7. Jones, p. 65.

8. McCrory, p. H5.

9. Karen Kennedy, "Cheerleaders, Mariachis Greet City's Outstanding Young Man," *San Antonio Express-News*, January 18, 1981, p. A2.

10. Jones, p. 65.

11. Cisneros, p. 26.

Chapter 6

1. Kemper Diehl and Jan Jarboe, *Cisneros: Portrait of a New American* (San Antonio, Tex.: Corona Publishing Company, 1985), p. 155.

2. Kemper Diehl and Jan Jarboe, "Prince of the City," *San Antonio Express-News*, April 14, 1985, p. M1.

3. Carmina Danini, "Cisneros' Parents Spend Day in Joyous Celebration," *San Antonio Express-News*, December 18, 1992, p. A2.

Chapter 7

1. Stephen Harrigan, "The Time of His Life," *Texas Monthly*, September 1987, p. 136.

2. Henry Cisneros, "San Antonio: Laying the Foundation For the Future," *USA Today*, July 1987, p. 24.

3. Sophronia Gregory, "Most Hearts Go Ker-Thump," *Time*, June 21, 1993, p. 17.

4. Harrigan, p. 142.

5. Ibid.

6. Daniel Pedersen, "I Am Not Perfect," *Newsweek*, October 24, 1988, p. 25.

7. "Mary Cisneros Says Her Faith Helps Her Cope," *Houston Post*, October 18, 1988, p. A14.

8. Marty Graham, "Her Life's in Ruins, Cisneros' Former Mistress Says," *Houston Post*, August 8, 1994, p. A8.

9. Pederson, p. 25.

10. Susie Phillips, "City Leaders: SA Progress, Change a Reflection of Mayor," *San Antonio Express-News*, May 28, 1989, p. J3.

11. Richard Smith, "Texas Legislators Recall Cisneros Drive, Charisma," *San Antonio Express-News*, May 28, 1989, p. J3.

12. Jan Jarboe, "Back to the Past," *Texas Monthly*, April 1990, p. 132.

Chapter 8

1. Roger Hernandez, "Hispanic Organizations Searching For Unity," *Hispanic*, September 1991, p. 19.

2. Nancy Jacobs, ed., *Into the Third Century* (Wylie, Tex.: Information Plus, 1992), p. 13.

3. Carol Foster, ed., *Minorities* (Wylie, Tex.: Information Plus, 1992), p. 108.

4. Stefanie Asin, "Census Deflates Hispanic Clout," *Houston Chronicle*, July 7, 1993, p. P13.

5. "More Hispanics Enrolling in Colleges," *Houston Chronicle*, November 5, 1993, p. A10.

6. Mark Siegel, ed., *Social Welfare* (Wylie, Tex.: Information Plus, 1992), p. 17.

7. "Election '92," *Time*, November 16, 1992, p. 19.

8. Robert Suro, "Cisneros Achieves Career Comeback With Nomination," *The New York Times*, December 18, 1992, p. A32.

9. Jan Jarboe, "About Face," *Texas Monthly*, March 1993, p. 116.

Chapter 9

1. United States Senate Committee on Banking, Housing and Urban Affairs, Transcript of Confirmation Hearing of Henry Cisneros, January 13, 1993, p. 4.

2. Ibid., p. 8.

3. Johnson, Otto ed., *The 1994 Information Please Almanac* (New York: Houghton Mifflin Company), 1994, p. 44.

4. Cornelia Cessna, ed., *Growing Up In America* (Wylie, Tex.: Information Plus, 1993), p. 33.

5. Transcript, p. 42.

6. Ibid., p. 126.

7. T. H. Watkins, *The Great Depression* (New York: Little Brown & Co., 1993), p. 51.

8. John W. Kirshon, ed., *Chronicle of America* (New York: Chronicle Publications), p. 658.

9. Susan Kellam, "Public Housing," *Congressional Quarterly Researcher*, September 10, 1993, p. 801.

10. Jeffrey Katz, "Rooms For Improvement: Can Cisneros Fix HUD?" *Congressional Quarterly*, April 10, 1993, p. 920.

Chapter 10

1. Jeffrey Katz, "Rooms For Improvement: Can Cisneros Fix HUD?" *Congressional Quarterly*, April 10, 1993, p. 914.

2. Ibid., p. 918.

3. Michael Paulson, "Housing Department Spent Millions On Local Projects," *San Antonio Light*, December 18, 1992, p. A4.

4. Jan Jarboe, "About Face," *Texas Monthly*, March 1993, p. 117.

5. Henry Cisneros, Transcript of Speech to the National Press Club, April 13, 1993, p. 5.

6. Susan Kellam, "Public Housing," *Congressional Quarterly Researcher*, September 10, 1993, p. 802.

7. Jeffrey Katz, "Domestic Battles," *Congressional Quarterly*, December 11, 1993, p. 147.

8. Richard Stewart, "HUD Takes Over Complex in Vidor," *Houston Chronicle*, September 15, 1993, p. A1.

9. "People," *U.S. News and World Report*, September 27, 1993, p. 17.

Chapter 11

1. Sophronia Gregory, "Most Hearts Go Ker-Thump," *Time*, June 21, 1993, p. 17.

2. Beth Wagner, "Cisneros' Son Admitted For Heart Surgery," *Houston Chronicle*, July 2, 1993, p. 16.

3. "Cisneros Vows to Transform HUD Into Activist Agency," *Houston Post*, October 14, 1993, p. A23.

4. Jill Smolowe, "Giving the Cold Shoulder," *Time*, December 6, 1993, p. 29.

5. "Public Health Programs and Practices," *Public Health Reports*, July/August 1993, p. 521.

6. Smolowe, p. 28.

7. Ibid., p. 29.

8. "HUD to Help Homeless," *Houston Chronicle*, December 4, 1993, p. A22.

9. Bennett Roth and Greg McDonald, "President Discloses $411 Million to Aid the Homeless," *Houston Chronicle*, December 23, 1993, p. A2.

10. Laurie McGinley, "HUD's Cisneros Has Big Plans, Firey Charisma, Clinton's Ear—and a Few New Sources of Funds," *The Wall Street Journal*, April 20, 1993, p. A22.

Chapter 12

1. Mark Horvit, "Cisneros Won't Seek U.S. Senate Position," *Houston Post*, December 15, 1993, p. A26.

2. Kathy Kiely, "Cisneros Sought OK From Boss," *Houston Post*, December 20, 1993, p. A27.

3. Ibid.

4. Terri Langford, "Black Family in Vidor Finds Hugs, Not Hate," *Houston Chronicle*, February 6, 1994, p. A17.

5. Ibid.

6. Lindsey Tanner, "Witness to Terror," *Houston Chronicle*, April 12, 1994, p. A2.

7. "Target: Housing Project Crime," *Houston Chronicle*, February 5, 1994, p. A12.

8. "Cisneros: 'Massive' Substandard Housing Plagues San Antonio," *Houston Chronicle*, December 28, 1993, p. A14.

9. Ibid.

10. Cisneros, Henry, "Rights and Responsibilites: The Health of the Urban Policy," *Vital Speeches*, June 15, 1994, p. 523.

11. "The 50 Most Beautiful People in the World," *People Weekly*, May 9, 1994, p. 98.

12. Ibid.

13. Susan Kellam, "Public Housing," *Congressional Quarterly Researcher*, September 10, 1993, p. 810.

14. Henry Cisneros, Transcript of Speech to the National Press Club, April 13, 1993, p. 5.

Further Reading

Callihan, Jeanne. *Our Mexican Ancestors.* San Antonio, Tex.: University of Texas Institute of Texan Cultures, 1981.

Coil, Suzanne. *The Poor in America.* Englewood Cliffs, N.J.: Julian Messner, 1989.

Diehl, Kemper, and Jan Jarboe. *Cisneros: Portrait of a New American.* San Antonio, Tex.: Corona Publishing Company, 1985.

Dunn, Wendy, and Janet Morey. *Famous Mexican Americans.* New York: Cobblehill Books, 1989.

Fernandez-Shaw, Carlos. *The Hispanic Presence in North America.* New York: Facts On File, 1987.

Harrigan, Stephen. "The Time of His Life." *Texas Monthly,* September 1987, pp. 86–91ff.

Jarboe, Jan. "About Face." *Texas Monthly,* March 1993, pp. 100–103ff.

Smolowe, Jill. "Giving the Cold Shoulder." *Time,* December 6, 1993, pp. 28–31.

Index

A
ACCESS, 104–105
Alamo, 4, 8, 43
All American City Award, 51

B
Bentsen, Lloyd, 84, 107

C
California earthquake of 1994, 111
Cisneros Assets Management Company, 72
Cisneros, Elvira Munguia, 10, 15
Cisneros, George, 10, 15–16
Cisneros, Henry.
    Central Catholic High School, 18–21
    city council, 36–40
    early years, 10–17
    George Washington University, 30, 34
    Harvard University, 33–34
    Little Flower Catholic School, 11, 14, 18
    marriage, 30
    mayor, first term, 42–50
        second term, 51–62
        third term, 62
        fourth term, 62–73
    Model Cities Program, 27–29
    National League of Cities, 32
    secretary of HUD, 5, 7, 8, 9, 86, 92–99, 101–106, 108–113
    Texas A&M University, 21–27
    vice-presidential candidate, 60
Cisneros, John Paul, 65–68, 70, 75, 82, 100–101
Cisneros, Mary Alice Perez, 19, 25, 30–31, 34–35, 37, 52, 58, 65–67, 71, 82, 83
Cisneros, Mercedes, 37, 52, 58, 66, 67, 75, 82
Cisneros, Teresa, 32, 34, 52, 58, 66, 67, 75, 82
Civil Rights Act of 1964, 98
Clinton, Bill, 5, 7, 79, 81–82, 113
Communities Organized for Public Service (COPS), 36
Conference on United States Affairs, 25
confirmation hearing, 84–86
Corps of Cadets, 22–23, 25
Cortes, Ernesto, 36

Creating Windows of
    Opportunity, 102

D

Democratic National
    Convention of 1984,
    53
Department of Housing and
    Urban Development
    (HUD), 5–6, 28,
    92–99
Díaz, Porfirio, 12

F

Ferraro, Geraldine, 60
Fiesta Texas, 74

G

Gore, Al, 79, 110
Governor's Task Force on
    Education, 54–56
Gramm, Phil, 85, 107
Great Depression, 6, 88

H

high-rise projects, 95–97
House Bill 72, 56–58
Hutchison, Kay Bailey, 107

I

illiteracy, 48

J

Jaycees Outstanding Young
    Man, 47
Johnson, Lyndon, 28

K

Kemp, Jack, 6, 7, 94

Kennedy, John F., 18–19
Ku Klux Klan, 98

L

League of United Latin
    American Citizens
    (LULAC), 76

M

migrant workers, 16
Model Cities Program,
    27–30
Mondale, Walter, 60
Munguia, Romulo, 11–12, 39

N

National Council of La
    Raza, 76
National Hispanic
    Leadership Agenda
    (NHLA), 76–77

O

Operation Safe Home, 110
One Stop Business Center,
    44

P

Pope John Paul II, 67, 69
poverty, 28, 44, 78, 85, 94
Presidential Committee on
    Federalism, 47
presidential election of 1992,
    80–81
public housing, 5–7, 86,
    88–90, 94

R

Reagan, Ronald, 45, 47, 51

Research Park Foundation, 61
Reserve Officer Training Corps (ROTC), 18, 26
Richardson, Elliot, 33
Rivercenter Mall, 61, 69, 74, 93
Robert Taylor Homes, 95–96, 107
Rockwell, Norman, 13
Roosevelt, Franklin, 6, 88

S
San Antonio, Texas, 8, 28, 43, 64, 69, 110
Sea World of Texas, 62, 69, 74
single member districts, 36, 39–40
Steen, John, 42

T
Target '90, 48, 62, 102
Today Show, 42

U
unemployment, 88–89
United States Housing Authority, 6, 89

V
Vidor Villa, 98–99, 108–109
voucher program, 96–97